Dyspraxia
2nd Edition

The SEN series

Dyspraxia
2nd Edition

Geoff Brookes

continuum

Continuum International Publishing Group

The Tower Building
11 York Road
London
SE1 7NX

80 Maiden Lane,
Suite 704
New York
NY 10038

www.continuumbooks.com

First published 2005
This second edition published 2007

British Library Cataloguing-in-Publication Data
A catalogue record for this book is available from the British Library.

ISBN: 0 8264 9235 5 (paperback)

Library of Congress Cataloguing-in-Publication Data
A catalog record for this book is available from the Library of
Congress.

Typeset by Servis Filmsetting Ltd, Manchester
Printed and bound in Great Britain by Antony Rowe Ltd,
Chippenham, Wiltshire

Contents

Dyspraxia

Contents

Foreword

Dyspraxia is such a frustrating condition. It has few physical manifestations but it has the capacity to determine the shape of someone's life and to turn a family upside down. Yet because it cannot be seen, some find it hard to believe that it is a genuine condition. They say it is made up, an invention to explain away under-achievement.

Live with a dyspraxic though and you will soon change your mind. You will see a child desperately trying to clutch at life through a veil of fog, always finding that the world is moving faster than they are; always finding that the things they want are, tantalizingly, just out of reach. Oh yes, dyspraxia is real enough and terribly frustrating for everyone who comes into contact with it, whether at home or at school.

This book is only an introduction to a complex condition. There is so much more to say. All I can do is give you a flavour of what it is like and to direct teachers to practical advice that might be of real benefit to dyspraxic children. It is no more than they deserve.

I dedicated the first edition of this book to my son David who has dyspraxia. He taught me so much about the condition. It is true to say that without him I wouldn't have written this work. As this second edition

Dyspraxia

is being prepared David is busy with his final school examinations. University beckons. His spirit and courage through all the hard years have been remarkable. The condition might be exhausting and frustrating, but never let it win. My son didn't.

So David, this second edition is dedicated to you as well.

Introduction

Dyspraxic children are lazy
Dyspraxic children are stupid
Dyspraxic children just need to work harder
Dyspraxic children are naughty and disruptive
Dyspraxic children are created by bad parenting
Dyspraxic children just need to concentrate a bit more
Dyspraxic children will eventually grow out of it

All these statements are wrong.

They are myths, but persistent ones, and reflect the reluctance of some people to accept the reality of the condition. It is much more straightforward to deny that it exists. When you do that, then you don't have to seek out solutions. You don't need to try to understand. It is easier to say that it is nothing more than an excuse for poor behaviour and for inadequate family circumstances. It is simpler to convince yourself that it is a posh excuse from middle-class parents looking for reasons why their child is letting them down. 'For goodness sake, pull yourself together. The only thing wrong with you is that you aren't very good at anything.' Thankfully those are days are passing. The condition is a real one, with a history and certainly with a future.

Dyspraxia

Dyspraxia has been called many things in its time. It is probably more accurately described as Developmental Coordination Difficulty, but for the purposes of this book I shall use the term dyspraxia. I am pleased to say that it is a term which is being used far more frequently as professionals in all fields show more willingness to engage with the implications of the condition. That in itself is an interesting point. Dyspraxia is a condition that calls upon the attention of so many differently skilled professional specialists; it can never be said to be a straightforward condition. You can't put it in a conveniently labelled box and then call the dyspraxia man to come and fix it.

Dyspraxia refers to the way in which the brain works in a different and less precise way for some people than it does for others. No one really knows why this should be. The dyspraxic's inabilities cannot be explained by events like a brain injury. It is there for no apparent reason. All you can say is that the organization of planned movement isn't successful: it is impaired.

Of course, there are those who claim that they do understand where it comes from and more importantly, who claim to be able to offer cures, but I am afraid that at the time of writing (January 2006) there is little substance for such claims. Until we can send a miniaturized man inside your head with a special welder to repair all the dodgy connections, there is nothing you can do to get rid of it. Once you've got it, you must learn to deal with it. And in most cases the condition can be managed, as long as it is approached with awareness and sympathy.

As our knowledge about the brain, and how messages are carried within it, grows, so does our understanding of what happens when things go wrong. It is impossible to define what is normal within something as rich and complex as the brain, but certainly the dyspraxic child has identifiable difficulties that the rest of us would not want to share. There are symptoms, there are problems, there are frustrations, there are tears. There are also strategies that can lead to positive outcomes. While it is important to understand where dyspraxia comes from, providing support and guidance for both children and their parents is what this book is all about. It attempts to ensure that teachers are informed about the condition and, more importantly, enable them to acquire the strategies to provide effective help to the dyspraxic children in their care. They are special children. They have so much that they can offer the future. They have talents, determination, and a different way of looking at the world. Theirs is a vision that we would be wrong to sacrifice.

They need our help if they are to make the kind of contribution to the world that they should. As professional and committed teachers, we should all be prepared to offer that help.

1

What is Dyspraxia?

Developmental dyspraxia is a neurologically based disorder, which means it happens within the brain where we cannot see it. It is a motor-planning difficulty that is present from birth. The Dyspraxic Foundation offers a useful definition: it is 'an impairment or immaturity in the organization of movement which leads to associated problems with language, perception and thought' (1999). There is significant disruption to the things that a person is trying to do. Dyspraxic subjects will have poor understanding of the messages that their senses convey and will experience difficulty in relating those messages to appropriate actions. Physical activities are hard to learn and hard to remember.

What appears to happen is that parts of the motor cortex in the brain do not develop properly. This prevents messages from being transmitted efficiently to the body, so dyspraxics have difficulty in planning movement to achieve a predetermined idea or purpose. Basically the dyspraxic child cannot make their body do what they want it to do quickly enough. Actions can be carried out but not instinctively and with little conviction. Connections appear to be either missing or disrupted. This must be extremely frustrating.

Dyspraxia

Technically speaking it is a disorder of these three processes within the brain:

1 Ideation – forming the idea of using a known movement to achieve a planned purpose.

2 Motor planning – planning the action needed to achieve this idea.

3 Execution – carrying out the planned movement.

Here are examples of three types of dyspraxia to help clarify this:

Oral dyspraxia

A child will not be able to reproduce mouth movements. So if they were asked to put their tongue in their cheek they would be unable to carry out the instruction, even though they could do it unconsciously.

Verbal dyspraxia

A child will have difficulty in making sounds or in forming words out of sounds. So when trying to say 'ship' they might say 'bip', no matter how hard they try. This is because there is an immaturity of the speech production area of the brain.

Motor dyspraxia

This prevents a child moving in a planned way. They know that they want to catch a ball but they cannot organize the necessary movements to achieve this.

The ball hits them in the chest before they can order and arrange their hands to receive it.

Oral dyspraxia and verbal dyspraxia are also known as the childhood apraxia of speech and there is a brief outline of this specialized area later in this book (see Chapter 8).

What is important is a recognition that dyspraxia may affect any or all areas of development – sensory, physical, intellectual, emotional, social or linguistic. And this lack of efficiency in delivering and receiving messages can happen in any of the millions of connections within the brain. Every dyspraxic person is different as a result.

2

The Science

If we understand the science then we will understand the origins of the condition. It is important to have a basic understanding of how the brain works in normal circumstances so that we can see where the problems might lie when things deviate from that norm. A significant volume of research is telling us more and more about how our brains function. And it is clear from this that the dyspraxic child is the victim of things over which they have no control at all, for the origins of the condition lie at the earliest stages of brain tissue development in the womb.

The brain is constructed and works as follows:

◆ It is made up of neurons which are connected by nerve fibres or axons to their various destinations in the body. They are arranged in lobes in those familiar two halves or hemispheres.

◆ There are four lobes in each hemisphere – the frontal, parietal, temporal and occipital lobes.

◆ Different functions of the body are controlled by different parts of the brain.

Dyspraxia

♦ 'Messages' and information travel along nerve fibres by way of the spinal cord, cortex, cerebellum and the corpus callosum.

♦ Incoming information from the senses – touch, taste, sight, smell, hearing, movement, balance, warmth, language, experience, sense of self – is organized and stored in the brain, to be retrieved for use as it is needed.

♦ The part of the brain which deals with basic emotions and instinctive actions is called the limbic system.

It is no surprise that minor disruptions to something so complex can have far-reaching and unpredictable consequences. This disruption, which can cause dyspraxia among other things, can happen as the brain develops in the womb, though no causes for such problems have yet been convincingly identified. A weakness, an unexpected connection or the absence of a connection can be established at any time.

The pre-birth growth of a baby goes through clearly defined developmental stages. From the moment of conception the fertilized egg divides and multiplies. Some cells will separate from the rest and continue to multiply at their own increased rate to become the nerve cells (neurons) of the brain. After six months' gestation the neurons, with their axons, have been produced and subsequently no further new neurons are grown. Furthermore, they do not regenerate. This is an important point. A neuron that is damaged, or dies, or does not complete its growth and thus reach its destination, will not be replaced or renewed, unlike cells in other parts of the body. Thus, if a nerve cell of the brain or group of cells fails to complete its growth and reach its destination, future sensory information from that area will be impaired. A route will not be established; a connection will not be formed; it won't work as it should. This idea of connections not quite reaching the right destination is a crucial point in understanding dyspraxia. This system failure can happen in any part of the brain, whether that part deals with movement, speech or emotion. Hence the wide-ranging nature of dyspraxia.

A development that does continue, and indeed does so into old age, is that of the individual cells. They grow dendrites. These are branches that reach out and form connections within the brain. There are billions of neurons in every brain, each with many connections with other cells. The infinite number of such combinations is what makes every brain unique.

For correct operation, neurons have to develop in sufficient numbers in the right areas of the brain and they must extend to the correct destination. This has to be achieved by the appropriate developmental stage or it will never occur.

There are two kinds of neurons – those carrying messages to the brain (sensory) and those carrying messages from the brain (motor). The implications of inappropriate development in either direction are obvious and suggest the ways in which messages can be disrupted. After six months' gestation the axons begin to develop an insulating fatty sheath called myelin. This is important because it allows messages to be carried efficiently along them. The best analogy is that it functions rather like the insulation around an electric wire. Without it the messages or impulses would fly around everywhere. The myelin makes sure that the messages are concentrated and heading for the correct destination. It takes time for this protective sheath to be completed. It is in place at around three months of age; babies younger than that will make random reactive movements, without purposeful intent. After myelination, movements will slowly become more deliberate, with a purpose and intent. The eyes may become more focused, and the baby may recognize, or touch, a face and smile. The development of the myelin sheath explains why young children tend to be clumsy and also why some professionals are reluctant to give an early diagnosis of dyspraxia. We all go through a stage when we exhibit some of the symptoms, but it is a stage that most of us leave behind as our brains mature.

The successful creation of such secure message paths is a vital part of our development. It is interesting to note that multiple sclerosis is a direct result of a partial breakdown of the myelin sheath and message-carrying capacity.

The connections between nerve cells, dendrites, which are connecting branches, and synapses, which are minute gaps across which impulses pass, continue to increase throughout a lifetime – their development stimulated by the demands of the environment, by relationships, experiences and as learning takes place. Every brain is different, with a unique set of connections. These are the things that make all of us so very different and which give rise to our personal contribution to the world around us. No one sees the world in exactly the same way. This is the basis for a person's sense of humour. A unique and surprising connection is made between thoughts or events. It is something that hasn't occurred to us before, but someone else has seen it. Why didn't we?

Why is one person good at languages and their sister a star tennis player who can barely string two words together? How can twin brothers both become international football players but with different levels of skill? Because our brains are organs of staggering complexity with an infinite set of possible connections within them. In some people certain connections are securely established; in others they are not.

Cultural influences upon us make us speak with similar accents and demonstrate similar characteristics that serve to distinguish people brought up in Eire from those living in Italy. But our different brain connections make each of us very different people. Our brains can process large volumes of information in an individual way. They are involved in a huge amount of traffic every day and if messages, like trains, can't get through straightaway then they have to be re-routed. Hence delays and disruption when there are neurological leaves on the line.

Indeed the idea of a railway network is perhaps a good way of getting hold of the concept of dyspraxia and may prove a useful comparison to share with a dyspraxic child who is anxiously trying to understand what is happening to them. There are all these messages whizzing round the brain on special tracks and sometimes there is something blocking the line. So the message goes the long way round. It needs to find a different way into the station.

Dyspraxia

Praxis

The term 'dyspraxia' comes from the Greek word 'praxis', which means doing, acting, deed or practice. Praxis is central to us as human beings. It links what goes on in our heads with what we actually do. It enables us to function in our world by linking the brain and behaviour, so we can dress, eat with cutlery, write, catch a ball, swim. These are not instinctive actions; they are things that we plan to do. We don't make a cup of tea at an instinctive level. We think through a series of actions. Most animals don't have a great deal of praxis. It is one of the essential things that makes us what we are; it makes us human beings.

Praxis develops as connections are refined in the brain. As we grow, we carry out actions of increasingly better quality, allowing us to do things that are more complicated. Look at babies. They begin by making largely uncontrolled movements, waving arms and legs around without much of a purpose. Soon these actions are controlled by the will and carried out with premeditated purpose, in order to touch a rattle, or to look at their mother. This involves some motor planning, some praxis. These actions are not random or accidental. The child is recalling previous actions and repeating them, modelling what it does now on what it successfully achieved before. Actions soon become more complicated as the brain acquires more retrievable memory of movement sequences. It can access these patterns with increasing success and efficiency.

Learning to talk requires us to organize a specific combination of muscles to produce the right controlled collection of sounds in the right sequence at the appropriate time to achieve a planned purpose (see Chapter 8 on Apraxia). This is praxis, and this is the source of the problem for dyspraxics. The brain sends out a message but it either never arrives or it staggers into the station after the moment has passed.

What goes wrong?

Let's go back to the three processes involved in carrying out an action, because if we look at how an action happens, we can see where it goes wrong for the child with dyspraxia.

Ideation

If a child comes across some wooden blocks for the first time it must gather as much information about them as possible. What shape are they? How do they feel? What do they taste like? How do they behave? Are they stable or mobile? That information has to be collected, arranged and stored. Then, when required, it can be retrieved and the knowledge of that experience can be used to form the idea of building something with the blocks. The child knows that they are stable and flat and that they sit together happily. Now, to build something with them the child will need a plan of action.

Motor planning

This planning happens in the parietal lobe of the brain. When it receives the idea, the 'planning department' has to work out and plan the instruction it has received.

Which part of the body should be where? Which particular muscles should contract or relax? In what sequence and by how much? It needs to remember the experience that was gathered about these blocks. This will refine the instructions it is about to send out – concerning the weight of the blocks, the size, etc. – and determine the sequence in which the muscles are to work. Then it is time to send out the messages for action.

Execution

Muscles can only either contract or relax in response to messages received from the brain telling them what to do, for how long and in what order. Messages then travel back from the muscles to the brain so that the action can be monitored and revised.

When you see the process broken down in this way then it seems a wonder anything ever happens at all. It appears so complex. The simple act of stirring a cup of tea seems impossible. If there were sand at the bottom of the cup then the muscles in your hand would flash a message back to the planning department and, if they are not out to lunch, they would work out what was going on by comparing this experience with a previous one. For instance: 'Something feels wrong. It is not like it was when I stirred it before. It is not dissolving like sugar . . .' and so on. Information is flying backwards and forwards all the time while the situation is assessed. It is not long before a conclusion is formed.

The three stages are interdependent and they rely for the success of any action upon the messages travelling on the correct tracks and making the correct connections. If anything interrupts the messages or if the planning department is indeed out to lunch and the brain can't recall quickly enough doing this action before, then the process will be disrupted. That is what dyspraxia does.

The way in which we learn is a stratified process. Certain skills must be mastered first and then other skills can be added on top of them: we learn to count first and only then can we begin to learn how to add and subtract. So any disruption in the learning process for any skill will affect the subsequent mastering of later skills that depend upon it. It is not that a dyspraxic child will never be able to learn things. It is that it will take them so much longer to do so, with lots of stops and starts along the way.

What happens when praxis fails?

In the complex system of information gathering and delivery, something is going wrong. The messages are not getting through or are not producing the right results. Who knows what is happening? Perhaps the information was not collected or transmitted or stored properly. Perhaps it was stored in the wrong place. Perhaps it was taken out and then put back in the wrong place – and we all know how frustrating that can be. Perhaps the planning department didn't send the messages to the right destination. Perhaps the right nerve fibres are missing or are incomplete. Whatever is happening the praxis is failing, so the child may not be able to pick up the bat quickly enough to hit the ball, or it may not be able to work out how to move from chewing to swallowing. This is also why it can be such an inconsistent condition. Yesterday the messages were getting through, the information was retrieved and the task completed. They could colour in the clown without straying outside the lines. Today the plan has been lost, the filing system has broken down, and the information put back in the wrong place. They can't colour in the clown. Of course the file may turn up again tomorrow, or the child may have to relearn the skill.

Colouring in is a simple example, but there could be a system malfunction at any location in the brain. Just imagine how complicated things can become if there is a problem in the area that sorts out relationships and emotions. You cannot approach anything with confidence.

In these instances where praxis fails, incoming signals from the environment are not switched automatically to the correct place but must search through a mass of dendrites and may use a tangle of pathways instead of selecting the correct one.

This explains why dyspraxic children use lots of unnecessary movement. It is quite possible that messages could be travelling to all four limbs instead of the one or two necessary to complete an action. It is interesting to note that assessments which ask dyspraxic children to walk on the outside of their feet show them curling their arms up in front. This shows there is a dodgy connection that links these two actions within their brains but not inside anyone else's.

There may also be delay at the synapses. This explains the pause in responding to instructions which many dyspraxic children show and the characteristic poor coordination they exhibit when different body parts have to be used together or in sequence. There is just too much traffic to be dealt with efficiently. All the information is piling in at one end but it needs to be sorted out and the motor responses required emerge from this jumble rather too slowly. As far as the poor brain is concerned, it simply cannot get the staff.

3

Question Time

Is dyspraxia new?

Of course not, it has existed for as long as the brain has been operating. The brain is such a complex organ it is hardly a surprise that parts of it are wired up differently. Those brain connections make us individuals. Why is one person good at billiards and their brother absolutely useless? Why is handwriting so unique? How did Shakespeare write as he did? Why do some ideas leap into your mind from nowhere?

Our brains all work differently and they process all our different experiences, seeing insights, forming connections. If one part of the brain isn't talking successfully to another then things are bound to be unpredictable. Think about what happens when the different parts of your computer decide that they don't want to communicate with each other. Things fall apart very quickly and you get extremely frustrated. Welcome to dyspraxia.

Developmental dyspraxia was finally categorized by doctors in the twentieth century. It was originally described as 'congenital maladroitness'. In 1937, Dr Samuel Orton described it as 'one of the six most common developmental disorders, showing distinctive impairment of praxis'. Jean Ayres called it 'a disorder of sensory integration', in 1972. In 1975, Dr Sasson Gubbay called it 'Clumsy child syndrome'. It has been called other things too: developmental awkwardness, sensorimotor dysfunction, developmental coordination disorder. Today, the World Health Organization lists it as the 'specific developmental disorder of motor function'. It has lots of names but they all mean the same thing. What is far more important than a label, however, is the help and understanding a child receives from those around them which can help them manage this condition.

What are the symptoms?

It doesn't have a common set of symptoms, so it is not what doctors call a unitary disorder like scarlet fever or mumps, where everyone suffers in the same way. Each person is affected in different ways and to different degrees.

The fact that each child is affected differently is hardly a surprise given the complexity of the brain and its workings. Naturally, in the majority of cases, parents notice it first. Developmental stages in the child may not be reached or negotiated; the child may be late in learning to sit, stand or walk. As far as crawling is concerned, some dyspraxic children never manage it at all. If this particular inability is noted, it can represent a defining moment.

The reason why many children later diagnosed as dyspraxic never crawl is because the required skills of coordination, sequential movement and balance are just too difficult for them to master. Crawling is not just a touching and memorable moment for happy parents;

it is an important skill. It involves balancing in a safe prone position, stretching out in different directions at the same time and, as a result, learning about positioning in space as well as learning to coordinate all four limbs to achieve a predetermined purpose. Unfortunately, an inability to crawl affects the acquisition of other skills such as throwing, catching and climbing, because they also require balance and timing and spatial orientation. There are those who go further and claim that this early lack of sequencing practice inhibits reading, pointing out that many dyslexic children never learn to crawl either.

Other expected skills may not be mastered. An early indication may be feeding difficulties. The child may not be able to coordinate swallowing efficiently and may later prove to be a messy eater who spills things all the time or is especially inefficient at dressing themself. Shoelaces may prove to be an impenetrable mystery. The routine tasks of daily life may prove impossible.

Here are some other symptoms but do remember, this is not an exhaustive list:

♦ irritability and poor sleep patterns

♦ poor writing and drawing ability

♦ inability to stay still

♦ difficulty in going up and down hills

♦ a lack of rhythm

♦ short attention span

♦ difficulty in carrying out instructions

- ◆ frequently falling and bumping into things
- ◆ poor posture and fatigue
- ◆ too trusting, with little sense of danger.

If I haven't got it now, does it mean that I am safe?

No, it doesn't. It is possible to suffer from acquired dyspraxia, which occurs after damage to the brain. It could be the result of a stroke, an accident or a medical disaster. This usually happens to older people and the difference from the way it affects children is that they have a memory of praxis that they will need to restore. The machine might have crashed but the information is in there somewhere. You can reboot and rescue it. Children with developmental dyspraxia don't have this lost or damaged memory to recover. For them the brain is, literally, immature.

What causes it?

It is not the result of poor physical strength. It is not a deformity. It does not show up under neurological examination. In spite of all the research in recent years and the raised profile that it has, the causes cannot be clearly identified. There may be an inherited tendency that predisposes members of a family to this and other conditions.

If there is a history of dyspraxia on the mother's side there is a one in three chance of it being passed on. If the history is on the father's side, then the likelihood is almost two in three. But not all children with dyspraxia have such family traditions and other factors have been implicated. There may have been a momentary problem – an illness, a lack of oxygen at a crucial stage of foetal development or at birth – that caused the damage. Maternal stress during pregnancy has also been implicated. Or it could simply be that particular connections between cells are faulty. The fact that it can coexist with other disorders such as dyslexia or attention deficit disorder means that precise diagnosis can be difficult, since all the symptoms intermingle.

The dyspraxic's inability to plan and sequence thought and to predict outcomes is a symptom of a problem deep inside the brain. This is the predictable answer to the question about where it comes from. But the real answer is that it is nothing much more than a roll of the dice.

Who gets it?

The condition affects up to 4 per cent of the population but at least 70 per cent of those affected are male. Sufferers are generally of average or above average intelligence. Teachers can therefore assume that there is at least one child with the condition in every class. Of course, in specialist provision the incidence could well be over 50 per cent. Remember, too, that only those children where the disorder seriously impairs learning or development are ever properly diagnosed. There are many others who are not recognized and instead are given other labels – like thick or slow or clumsy. If you start thinking of difficult boys in classes that you have met, you might be able to see some of the symptoms of dyspraxia in the behaviour they have displayed. It is clear too that thinking about unpredictable developments within the structure and connections of the brain can also help you come to terms with the way some boys behave in lessons and around the school.

Poor achievement can lead to low self-esteem and antisocial behaviour. We have all seen this. Some now believe that three-quarters of children with behavioural difficulties have dyspraxia. Among those in young offenders' institutions the incidence is equally high.

Of course, not all dyspraxics become delinquent but they may indeed become disillusioned with an education system that seems to exclude them and seek out other areas of interest. Schools and teachers need to do their jobs properly and provide them with the support that will help them build successful lives.

How is it diagnosed?

Occupational therapists, physiotherapists, speech therapists, teachers, psychologists, educational psychologists or paediatricians can perform tests to diagnose dyspraxia. But it is the parents of the child who usually carry out the most effective initial diagnosis. They will know that something is wrong; they may not realize what it is but they will know that something isn't right. They will have noticed difficulties and developmental surprises, perhaps from very early on in the child's life. A weak sucking reflex is often an early indicator. The child will appear healthy and alert and there may be no obvious explanation for the difficulties they are facing.

Dyspraxia may exist in isolation or as part of, or as a symptom of, another disorder which makes diagnosis difficult. Once other disorders have been excluded and dyspraxic signs and symptoms identified, then a diagnosis is usually possible. It is often the case, however, that a diagnosis is only made when a child starts school.

So what happens next?

When a child is diagnosed with dyspraxia they should be assessed by an educational psychologist with a view to a statement of special educational needs being drawn up. An Individual Education Plan (IEP) will help everyone. It will help teachers to respond to, and plan for, children who are often very talented. It might offer advice to parents about strategies and may suggest possible dietary supplements such as evening primrose oil and fish oils which some have found effective. The IEP will be essential in guaranteeing the dyspraxic child the extra time in examinations that is their right. Achievement in examinations will have long-lasting consequences.

Most importantly, both the statement and the subsequent IEP will reassure the child that they are not alone and that their needs and frustrations have been recognized. There are things that will help. It will also reassure parents that their concerns are being taken seriously.

There is another important point here too. There is a good chance that the child will proceed to further or higher education. A statement of special educational needs has consequences for funding and might trigger important support for a family in terms of grants and equipment and this should be explored.

Dyspraxia

What is needed at an institutional level is that the condition is treated with sympathy and from a position of knowledge. There should, ideally, be someone in every school, at every level, who knows something about it and can offer some advice. It is not an isolated condition; there are sufferers in every school, possibly in most classes, and statementing procedures are a significant means by which the profile of understanding can be raised. And when you think about the statistics, not only have you already taught a child with dyspraxia, but there is likely to be someone with the condition, in whatever form, in your extended family. How would you want them to be treated in their classroom?

4

The Dyspraxic Child

The first thing to say is that there are no physical attributes which distinguish them from anyone else. They do not carry a label that allows strangers to stare at them. A dyspraxic child will say with some justification, 'I am able bodied. I have full use of my arms and legs. I am not a freak. I am not confined to a wheelchair. I am no different to anyone else.' But they are different, and the condition affects every facet of the child's life. It goes way beyond inabilities with words or pens or physical movement. It might begin with movement but it will impact most profoundly on communication and social and emotional development. It is in these areas that the parents will need to confront major problems and fears. It is part of your role as an informed teacher to offer them reassurance, knowledge and support.

Dyspraxia exists in different degrees and in different combinations. The symptoms are not necessarily common. Thus the most effective remedies are those that are specific to each child because what they need is unique. Perhaps this has always been the case with all children, whether they have a problem or not, but there is certainly no place for a 'one size fits all' approach to dyspraxia.

Dyspraxia

Often, however, dyspraxic children are denied sympathetic handling because they are not visibly different. Their difficulties appear to some to be an affectation. As Doctor Amanda Kirby says (see Resources), 'It is a hidden handicap.' Even if we can't see it, dyspraxics do have a disability. Even if it is hidden from view it is still a real one. But if they are bright and well behaved then their problems are minimized and even overlooked – 'What's the problem? There's nothing wrong with them.' But the emotional issues will always lurk in the background, to be exacerbated by the cruel assaults on their self-esteem that daily life in school will mount.

They may find it difficult to build successful relationships within their own peer group. They might avoid group activities, preferring solitary play, and their lack of social skills might mean others can't accept them. They may be perceived as odd because their thought processes are different, making their conversation strained. The connections that others see as a conversation builds are not recognized and what they say can seem irrelevant. They can seem out of sync with everyone else and their behaviour can seem immature. The sort of relationships that boys establish – competitive and teasing – are hard for them to master since they are never sure which comments are real and which ones are jokes. When they eventually try to emulate the fundamental basis of male interaction, they usually get it wrong. They are unable to decode the social environment quickly enough.

As a result, the dyspraxic child is often a loner. He is often a boy who isn't very good at the things a boy is supposed to be good at. He will be poor at sport. Even simple things like kicking and throwing can be challenging.

Because of these experiences, their self-esteem will be a fragile thing indeed. A cross word or a family spat can leave them in pieces sobbing on the bedroom floor. The feeling that they might have disappointed their parents or teachers leads to heart-wrenching and disproportionate despair.

There are frequently additional problems with speech and the processes that underpin it. For a start, dyspraxia can alter the production of sounds because it can affect those muscles that control speech. The organization of language in the brain may be affected, so poor sequencing skills may alter the order of letters in words or the order of words within a sentence. A child could have difficulty in identifying the right sounds; imitating sounds, whistling, blowing balloons could all be impossible. It is not a surprise that a diagnosis of dyspraxia is often made by speech therapists. Naturally enough, if a child can't relate a letter or combination of letters to the sound it produces, they will struggle to grasp spelling patterns. Making the sounds themselves calls upon organization and coordination to move the muscles sufficiently in the correct sequence. If you can't manage this effectively what sort of sounds are you going to produce?

Words are often troublesome. If the child cannot find the right words quickly enough in their heads, then their ability to tell a story or to recount an event may become confused or lengthy. If they cannot organize their thoughts they will struggle to establish an order, so there could be lots of repetition, hesitations, false starts and it will require a great deal of effort. Others may draw disparaging conclusions from these problems. There are other dyspraxic children for whom the spoken word has fewer problems. Their difficulties emerge in writing.

All this is a genuine frustration for parents. Their child's developmental problems can seem to be a punishment for having a high IQ. They may have to work extremely hard to convince others that their child has talents and abilities, once the fog that surrounds them has been penetrated.

It wouldn't be unusual to find that the dyspraxic child can read very fluently to themself, with insight and comprehension, but finds it impossible to do so out loud. It is often the case with dyspraxic children that, as a result, inaccurate and hasty conclusions are drawn about their abilities which may have a lasting influence.

In the sensory area there could be symptoms too. The child might have a poor sense of touch or even an overdeveloped one, which could mean that certain textures are very difficult to deal with, such as mashed potatoes. Some dyspraxic children find having their hair brushed or cut very uncomfortable, they can also react strongly to having their nails cut. For them the sensations are felt much more severely than normal. Some children cry because it hurts so much. The labels on clothes have been known to cause extreme irritation. Such extreme sensitivity makes the world a harsh and a cruel place, particularly when others cannot understand it.

There are other dyspraxic children who can't bear to be touched at all, even brushing lightly against them can cause an overreaction. They might lash out – to the surprise of those around them. This unexpected behaviour marks them out as unusual and unpredictable. It might be that they cannot endure holding hands in a circle. Other children naturally feel rejected since they can't understand the reasons for the refusal and take it personally. Slowly they become someone to be avoided. So, while taking hands in a circle or in a line may sound like a simple instruction, to a dyspraxic child it can be truly miserable and painful. So what are they to do? Follow the instruction and be in pain or ignore it and be in trouble?

Odd. Naughty. Anti-social. Suddenly they have a label. None of this helps a dyspraxic child build bridges with others in their class and it can drive them into isolation.

It will not be a surprise to learn that buttons and, especially, shoelaces can be impossible because of an inability to judge where body parts such as fingers are at a particular moment. This is significant. A dyspraxic child will have no sense of placement. If they want to climb onto a chair, they will look to check where the supporting foot is in relation to the chair – they won't be able to sense its position. This is because their proprioceptors, or nerve endings in the muscles and skin, are not relaying information as they should. Quite simply, they don't feel that they can rely upon their body. Parts of it are never where they think they should be. As a result, they find it really difficult to orientate themselves in space with any efficiency. They thump around. They misjudge distances. Their positional sense is flawed. They are clumsy, untidy, ungainly. That child who is always sharpening their pencil because they press on it too hard could have dyspraxia. The end of the pencil and the paper are never quite where they thought they were.

Dyspraxia

Lots of actions are affected. Sitting down without looking involves a judgement of where the body is in relation to the chair and this, in turn, gives you additional information. It tells you how much strength or release of strength is required to carry out the movement properly. A child lifting a cup needs to know where and when to curl his fingers round the handle and how much strength to use so that the liquid does not spill.

Those, like yourself, with efficient proprioceptors will manage these things automatically. You don't often spill that cup of coffee and you certainly don't think about it every step of the way. In fact, you can pick up the cup and sit down on that chair behind you at the same time. A dyspraxic child will hold a cup against themselves for extra support and will have to look closely at the process at every stage to make sure that neither their body nor the cup betrays them. In their world the chair they are aiming to sit on is never where they thought it was.

They could also have problems in blocking out unwanted sounds in order to concentrate on a specific one. This perhaps provides a useful way of trying to understand what they face in their day-to-day lives. They are swamped by a flood of information that overwhelms them before they can process it. They can't cut out visual and/or auditory 'distractors' from the environment around them. While most of us learn to focus on important signals, those affected by dyspraxia can't ignore other distractors. So when children need to stop what they are doing and look elsewhere or when they constantly hear other sounds instead of the teacher, their concentration goes and it can be hard to restore.

Consequently, some noise-sensitive children will give up the struggle to hear clearly and disappear into their own imaginary worlds. Then, of course, they may be accused of lacking concentration, which is unfair, because the ordinary world, as we experience it, shouts them down. Where else can they go? The world inside their heads is so much easier. School can become such a struggle. They are obliged to focus on something that is slipping through their fingers and at the same time constantly rebuild a series of individual actions to achieve a particular purpose while working so much harder than the rest of us in order to do so. It is no wonder that they are exhausted when they come home from school; everything they do needs a strained and frustrating level of concentration.

When I run and kick a ball or when I am trying to hang a piece of wallpaper, I don't have to work out every individual movement separately. The action comes as a package and I can concentrate on it without having to worry about the rest of my senses being overwhelmed. I can call upon the collection of remembered actions to perform the task and continue a conversation or listen to the radio at the same time. It happens all the time – writing, washing, chopping carrots. There are things that we do every day, that we take for granted, that a dyspraxic child could find tremendously difficult – like stepping on and off an escalator. They can't move fluidly because the messages aren't getting there efficiently. If you are a dyspraxic then there is a thick veil between you and your place in the world.

Just think of the frustrations of being able to see instantly what you need to do but having always to persuade your muscles to catch up. A top-class cricketer has instant coordination between eye and hand. When you watch them in full flow, their anticipation and reactions appear almost magical. By the time the dyspraxic has worked anything out it is too late. It must feel as if you are in slow motion and the world is whizzing around at double speed and swamping you before you are ready.

Sometimes they can be physically aggressive, lashing out in frustration at family and friends and showing a complete inability to explain why they have acted as they have. You can imagine that living with a dyspraxic can be very trying. Their frustrations can take a number of forms. They demand the sort of patience that comes from knowledge and understanding, and a teacher can be best placed to provide this.

Families will need help in dealing with the misunderstandings of the ill-informed who will label their child as lazy or difficult.

♦ They will need reassurance and strategies.

♦ They will need to know that someone is interested and that they can put the difficulties they are facing as a family into a context.

♦ They will need to know that someone cares and recognizes the qualities of their child.

♦ In short, they might need an advocate.

Family is very important to the dyspraxic child. It should provide security and happiness, a haven from a complex and confusing world. Sadly this isn't always the case and difficulties can be magnified hugely if that security disappears with the collapse of a family. A dyspraxic child can certainly create tensions within a family unit because they are so demanding. They will need extra attention and their parents can expect to act as intermediaries between them and the outside world in a more sustained way than they will with their other children. Other family members – as well as the child themself – will need to understand the full implications of the condition. If it affects one child then the knock-on effects will impact on all family members.

A dyspraxic child might in fact be happiest when at home. It is predictable, safe and controlled. This is quite a contrast with the behaviour that many other teenagers display, who try to distance themselves from their parents. It is something else that marks them out as different.

What is quite possible is that because the real world is so frustrating and depressing, the dyspraxic child will retreat from it. Perhaps into a fantasy world or into a world of endless plans. What will happen in the future, what they will do, what they will become. This focus on the future as a means of escape does not mean that they are ever likely to achieve these things. Such a focus brings with it no practicalities or strategies to achieve goals or to realize plans. It is an imaginary world, peopled by imaginary friends, full of plans and schemes.

At examination time in particular it might be necessary to encourage them to focus upon the present. It is achievement now that could make their future attainable. Plans made need to be turned into reality – and the only way that will happen is through organization and planning – and, as we've noted, the dyspraxic child will need help to do this. Of course, in this they are no different from many of their peers. But with the dyspraxic it coexists with so many other symptoms and difficulties.

The emotional immaturity that comes with dyspraxia can extend childhood well into the teenage years. They give you unconditional love and reliance. They are emotionally fragile and can be easily hurt. A harsh or unkind word expressed in the heat of the moment can have a disproportionate effect.

Their interest and knowledge can be unexpected and astonishing. They can become obsessive about a topic or issue to the extent that it can dominate their lives. Yet they cannot always show sufficient concentration to achieve success in a conventional sense in school.

As a teacher it isn't long before you come to share their frustration. You know how intelligent they are, the talents that they have, yet everything has to be accomplished through grey, obscuring wisps of fog. They can see what they want to do, but it is too slippery. It is almost within their grasp but not quite there – they have to nail the jelly to the wall. Their intelligence makes them acutely aware of the implications of their condition; they know that they can't do things that others can. You need to make sure that they keep on trying.

You need to keep in mind this idea of an unconventionally wired brain. The information or the knowledge of how to carry out a specific action is in there somewhere, it has just been stored in the wrong drawer. You will never find your socks if you put them in your pants drawer. Perhaps this silly analogy can point us towards something sensible: you might be able to stop putting your socks in the wrong drawer if it is clearly labelled. That is what dyspraxic children sometimes need – a bit of basic organization. Simple solutions. They might not be able to fasten shoelaces but does that matter? Buy elastic-sided shoes or trainers. Why was Velcro invented? They will need other people to help them find such solutions.

If you stop to think about it, poor muscle coordination or inadequate signalling within the body could have some unpleasant consequences – think of toilets and toileting. Any part of your life and procedures can be affected. There are many things that a teacher needs to know, as they will be the first port of call for anxious parents, especially for those working in the early years.

Of course, teachers must not label every child who is occasionally clumsy or disorganized as dyspraxic. This is a huge disservice to the genuine sufferers who have many more issues to deal with than bumping into tables. Precious resources need to be directed to where they are most needed. This is only possible through effective identification. The work of trained specialists in a range of disciplines needs to be targeted effectively. A teacher who has daily contact with a dyspraxic child needs to recognize the symptoms and make a judgement about where help is needed. This call can only be made on the basis of knowledge that brings with it a range of remedial strategies.

We can all become hung up on the causes. We can explore brain function and development – it is the only way to achieve a full and detailed understanding of dyspraxia – but the causes will still remain unclear. What teachers need to do is to deal with the means by which we intend to manage the condition in the classroom so that we can assess the potential of each child and support the parents who are trying to manage a difficult domestic situation.

If you needed reminding, teaching is more than just a job. Teachers have the opportunity through their understanding and sympathy to influence lives in radical ways. Dyspraxics and their families need these things from you.

5

Behaviour

Some dyspraxic children negotiate school successfully. Some do not. For some school is an inescapable confrontation with inadequacy. They know they can't cope very well and they have to deal with this every day. It is not a satisfactory experience but they are forced to repeat it, seemingly without end. Behavioural issues can result.

Obviously they suffer from considerable internal conflict because of the difference between what they want to do and what they can achieve. Dealing with other people is also very frustrating and their condition can lead to real exclusion by their peers and a lack of understanding from adults. If, for example, they have a difficulty in following instructions, their request for them to be repeated could mean that they are accused of not listening. They can become frustrated and irritated by such perceived intolerance. The inability to concentrate can lead to similar unfortunate labelling.

The stress of being at school can lead to poor behaviour in response. Indeed some children can display temper tantrums because the world seems deliberately to misunderstand their condition. They might also carry with them a sense of guilt, because they feel that they are letting their family down by being like they are – a clumsy incompetent embarrassment.

By the time they progress through secondary school the result is likely to be that the student will decide to opt out of school. This shouldn't be a surprise. If they feel that their needs are neither recognized nor met, they may also feel isolated and forgotten and so eventually reject school. It is much easier to be a clown or to become a disaffected isolate in order to hide any limitations and avoid failure.

This is where the idea of dyspraxia being a 'hidden handicap' (Dr Amanda Kirby's words) starts to impact. Our society is ready to recognize needs for the physically disabled. Ramps and lifts are rightly provided for children in wheelchairs. No one would expect a deaf child to be able to sing in key or suggest that all they need to do is try harder. We would make sure that their needs were met and the necessary equipment made available.

Dyspraxic children are no different. Their condition needs to be recognized and a strategy developed to accommodate it. Emphasis needs to be placed upon success rather than failure. This is a common theme throughout this book – be positive. In this way, over time, you will contribute to dispersing the low self-esteem that develops among some dyspraxic children. You will also modify and improve their behaviour. But children with dyspraxia don't go to school on their own; they do not inhabit a vacuum. They go to school with lots of other children. Sadly, an issue with the behaviour of others might soon emerge, for dyspraxic children are frequently the victims of bullying.

Bullying

What parents might soon come to realize is that the dyspraxic child appears to have the word 'Victim' painted on their forehead. It is a sorry state of affairs indeed and there is no doubt that the issue of bullying will eventually come the way of the teacher.

Why should this happen? Why are dyspraxic children so frequently the victims of bullying? The answer lies in the nature of their dyspraxia, its consequences and the way that the dyspraxic child is perceived.

We've said before that they are often hopeless at ball games. In the overall scheme of things this is hugely unimportant. Except when you are a boy.

For it is on such a trivial basis that you are judged, and the skills of the dyspraxic child are certainly not going to enhance the success of any team. So they are not picked. And because they are excluded from such a defining activity, they can become isolated loners, easily picked on. The bullying will almost certainly begin in a verbal form as a response to their perceived oddness but it can soon take on physical expression.

However hopeless they might be, they can still see themselves as being just on the edge of becoming very good, for they know what they want to do. It is just that something gets in the way. Next time they will be fine. So they don't shut up about it, they keep putting themselves forward for the team. They crave acceptance. The others around them will eventually get fed up. They will already have decided that the dyspraxic child is hopeless, and a liability.

It is quite likely that they will be regarded as peculiar, simply because they don't fit a stereotype. It will often appear to their peers that they have not achieved the proper milestones. So their ability to look untidy, their hair, their posture, their walk, will all flash out signals – what they are just doesn't add up. Their written work can resemble a disaster, their work displayed can inspire derision, yet their general knowledge can be exceptional. So they might be seen as freaks, with any verbal facility resented. The dyspraxic's inability to control their emotions may lead to them being labelled as immature. This can be exacerbated by their obvious difficulties in basic areas like getting dressed, tying laces, eating.

The presence of verbal dyspraxia will make them less articulate or perhaps a little slower to express their thoughts. It is also possible that they prefer playing with children who are either younger or older than themselves. Their own peers are the ones they avoid – and they are the ones who establish reputations. From here it is but a short step to bullying. The dyspraxia might be the cause but the solutions and strategies that need to be adopted are no different to those employed in any other circumstances.

A school should establish clear-cut rules about how bullying should be dealt with. A support network needs to be provided and a mentoring scheme established. Remember a dyspraxic child will usually relate well to someone who is older.

Watch out for the obvious signs that bullying might be happening:

♦ the child walking alone in the playground

♦ the child who is isolated on school visits

♦ a shortage of Christmas cards

♦ not being invited to parties

♦ others being reluctant to sit by them

♦ bruises and scratches

♦ possessions disappearing

♦ a sudden deterioration in the quality of work and in verbal responses.

In the end, dyspraxic children are perceived as different. And sometimes the others in the pack will want to drive them out. As a teacher, you want to harness their potential and offer fulfilment and purpose that will transcend their difficulties. All some of their peers will want to do is to bite them.

They seem to be living in a different time from the rest of us, always that little bit behind. This is something that comedians have used for years – the character who is out of step, either mentally or physically, with everyone else around them. This comic model is well established. It can't be a surprise, therefore, if those who fit into this stereotype are derided and abused. They can find themselves the butt of everyone's attempts at humour because they always seem to be catching up with a world that is moving faster than they are. Yet it is also true to say that dyspraxic children are special, with a refreshing innocence and an engaging relationship with their work. They musn't be sacrificed to the mindless oafs with a new joke to try out. Teachers will need to show vigilance if dyspraxic children are to be given the space in which to succeed. Not to do so is to leave their potential unful-filled.

The emotional consequences of dyspraxia do need careful consideration. The world they try to inhabit can be difficult enough. Their days can be stressful. They live with frustration, anxiety and failure. Their self-esteem can be low. They may also have behaviour problems that these issues provoke. The inconsistent development of the brain can affect their emotional development too. The information they get from their experiences and senses may be impaired, so they may not be able to understand their feelings.

They may show inappropriate emotions, or too much, so a small set-back can become a disaster. They can be too easily moved to tears. They can focus obsessively upon events like birthdays or holidays, repeating plans and ideas constantly until they appear to be real. They may pursue the repetition of questions and their answers as they try to fix an issue in their minds. This means that ordinary life as we all learn to come to terms with it can contain additional frustration and disappointment for them. These frustrations can make them seem immature and certainly emotionally fragile.

Without the consistent ability to read people and sit-uations or to recognize accepted behaviour, friendships may be difficult to form. So on the one hand, they want to keep up with their peers and to achieve success but on the other their behaviour will seem so odd. It is no surprise that they are frequently the victims of pro-longed bullying. Don't let it happen.

There is undoubtedly a touching level of sadness in the life of a dyspraxic child. Whatever they want always seems just outside their grasp. They need to be protected. Theirs is a hard enough road as it is.

Managing change

Dyspraxic children are not very good at managing change. The most stressful times for the dyspraxic are often the times of transition, when the child has to come to terms with major changes.

The times of change in anyone's life can be tricky periods to negotiate but for a child with dyspraxia they can be fraught with considerable danger. Just as one environment becomes familiar and can be negotiated carefully – allowances made, compensations established – things suddenly change radically. Familiarity is replaced by uncertainty. These are key occasions when parents should be especially aware and supportive and new teachers watchful. There needs to be careful communication. Change needs to be managed by an institution and by individuals. There are key transitions throughout the education system that need to be predicted and negotiated. The right people need to know the right things so that the dyspraxic child is treated with sympathy to ease this transition. It is one of those things that teachers need to do – to find out about the new children they are going to inherit and so be informed of any issues from the start.

Sadly, however much we may say otherwise, schools are not always effective when it comes to passing things on. So parents have every right to nag and pester if it ensures that the job gets done. After all, can they rely upon anyone else ever having their child's interests truly at heart?

6

Assessment and Diagnosis

You start off by asking yourself 'Why?'. Why bother? What is the point? You can't cure it. Just get on with it. But that would be wrong. Assessment is important. If a child is assessed as having dyspraxia then they are labelled. That labelling process can be a defining moment. It can trigger support and funding. With a label there comes an action plan. Suddenly parents can be reassured: your child isn't a freak. The problem has been identified, it will be taken seriously and consequently something will be done. You can find things out. You can talk to people with a similar difficulty. You can make things better.

This is, sadly, not always the case. One problem is that diagnosis isn't straightforward. One professional will say one thing and another might say the opposite. Get three of them in the room at the same time and you might have four opinions. There isn't a unified set of symptoms that can trigger a diagnosis. It is a diagnosis arrived at through the consideration of a number of factors. There is no one test or screening process that can identify the condition conclusively. A test is just part of a process.

So what might a professional be looking for? The basic criterion would be motor coordination that is significantly below the level expected, based on age and intelligence. This can be assessed by standardized tests.

Questions should be asked. How does the child interact with their environment? Is there a discrepancy between what happens and what you would normally expect? Any difficulties should have been present since early development and there will probably have been significant delays in achieving particular developmental milestones.

Any one of a range of specialists, including speech therapists and physiotherapists, could confirm difficulties seen by parents. Each of these honourable professions might hold an important part of the jigsaw, but generally in school an educational psychologist will probably make the diagnosis. They will need to look at the history of the child's problems and determine whether verbal skills are greater than physical skills to a significant degree. This would be an important conclusion, as we will see below.

The range and nature of the specific assessment tools used currently in the identification of dyspraxia lie outside the scope of this book. Tests are developed all the time. At the moment, the Weschler Intelligence Scale for Children (WISC) is most commonly employed. This can only be performed by a qualified psychologist. It contains a range of tests to measure verbal or performance ability. Areas like arithmetic, vocabulary and comprehension give a score for verbal IQ. Performance in things like picture completion, object assembly and design give a score for performance IQ. The results are combined to give a final IQ. A substantial difference between verbal IQ and performance IQ is a sign that dyspraxia may be present.

What is more important is that teachers should record any concerns they might have and pass them on to the educational psychologist. These will help to confirm judgements. It is clear that definitive assessment requires a detailed developmental history of the child and an informed teacher will make an important contribution here.

The WISC doesn't confirm dyspraxia. It is part of the picture. Particularly useful are observations on the child's behaviour during play. A great deal can be learned from this. In addition, has poor posture been noted? Are there difficulties in eye–hand coordination?

The psychologist will also employ motor-skills screening. This identifies any deficits and determines whether they actually form a pattern. For example, a child might have difficulties related to their right side. This would indicate that they have problems in the left hemisphere. The child will be observed walking on their toes backwards and forwards or on their heels for example. Their ability to stand still or on one leg or to throw and catch a large soft ball might be assessed.

A full picture needs to be formed. Obviously, the involvement of parents is vital, for they can provide an insight into the child's skills in daily life. Their observations are usually found to be honest and realistic. After all, they want the best for their child and are aware that something isn't quite right. They might not have been able to put a name to the condition, that's all. But to an experienced educational psychologist, the diagnosis of dyspraxia will be obvious.

This will all then contribute to a statement of educational needs. This will clarify the roles of everyone involved and spell out the nature of their responsibilities and obligations. It can also offer guidance to parents, areas to explore, who to contact, what to read. We all need to realize, however, that there is no quick fix, no magic potion. A statement will establish what the problem is and what it is not. It will focus resources but it won't offer a cure.

The best sort of assessment would involve both health services and education. It would examine the whole child, drawing together all the relevant information. It is logical to assume that coordination difficulties may lead to psychological problems and to poor motivation, concentration and then to social difficulties. So the whole picture is important, not just the separate symptoms.

The label that comes from the assessment will ensure that the difficulty is taken seriously. It is not that this is a new condition, far from it, but it is far more significant that it is now being recognized. The label will bring responsibility and focus. It will also bring people together who have similar problems and that can have so many benefits for everyone concerned. And it will, through the sharing of experience, allow people to adopt a more positive view. The diagnosis will concentrate on the things the child can't do. What you have to do as a teacher is to emphasize to parents and to the child what they can do. It is also important to reassure all concerned that they are not alone. With the label the assessments have provided you may access research and help forums. You can direct parents to appropriate levels of support. It was in finally discovering that our son had dyspraxia that we were able to react properly and with the right kind of support.

There can be no doubt that dyspraxia should be considered as a priority for resources, even within restricted budgets. There are many sufferers, many of them still undiagnosed. Their problems can be long-term and they can be intrusive. A sufferer can display poor social skills, low self-esteem, learning difficulties and behaviour problems. Even if you put on one side such concepts as responsibility and obligation, if no attempt is made to address these issues then the future demand on all manner of resources could be far greater. Remember that dyspraxia is recognized as a disability within the criteria established by the World Health Organization – there is an inability to carry out an activity within the range considered as normal. We need, as professionals, to respond to this and ensure the best for the children in our care. Without a proper and informed response, huge amounts of human potential will be unnecessarily sacrificed and lives will remain unfulfilled.

7

Physiotherapy

The baleful effects of dyspraxia are wide ranging as we can see and many different professionals can be involved in offering advice to a child. Each has their own role to play – educational psychologists, speech therapists, teachers. And where movement is involved, then the expertise of physiotherapists must not be overlooked. They can make an enormous contribution to the management of the condition and can develop strategies to effect real and measurable improvement. Just be aware, however, we are looking here at managing and improving the condition; we are not talking about a cure.

Paediatric physiotherapy has its own association (the Association of Paediatric Chartered Physiotherapists) and is concerned with 'the treatment of any childhood condition by physical means which threatens physical development and therefore may reduce full potential for adult independence'. It is clear from this, their own description of their important specialism, that they can have a big part to play in the managing of dyspraxia. If a child in your school is referred to a physiotherapist then they will receive treatment from someone who understands normal child development and normal movements. This places them in a good position to make judgements about the things that are not within normal parameters and they will know what they can do to help. Their focus will be to improve the quality of the child's movement through strategies such as exercises and games. The intention will be to build up self-confidence and self-esteem so that there can be wider learning benefits. They can bring a different perspective to that provided by the PE teacher, who, as we shall see, can have a huge influence, particularly on the development of dyspraxic boys (see Chapter 13). Physiotherapy is an avenue you should try to open up for any dyspraxic child in your classroom.

The classic symptoms of dyspraxia should be sufficient to justify a referral to a physiotherapist. What they will have to do is to assess where the greatest problems are. Are they exercising skills to an age-appropriate level or with the expected quality? They will assess things such as:

♦ Shoulder control, which is essential for hand control and thus for writing.

♦ Pelvic control, which is important in developing balance, hand–eye coordination and directional awareness.

♦ Midline crossing, which is the ability to cross one side of the body to the other, across an imaginary midline. It is something we do when we write or reach for things.

♦ Symmetrical integration, which is the ability to move both sides of the body simultaneously in an identical way, as we do when we catch something with both hands.

♦ Spatial awareness, which helps us to judge distances and our relationship with the objects around us.

Such skills and others are an integral part of the lives that we lead. When they don't go very well then important aspects of our lives don't go well either. So if you have poor performance in any of the skills associated with writing, such as shoulder control, hand–eye coordination, balance for sitting, midline crossing, spatial awareness, then your writing could be significantly impaired.

A physiotherapist will make their assessment using standardized tests and observations. Then they should draw up a programme of exercises based on the particular needs identified. They will set targets in discussion with the child and the parents. The programme might involve the child being seen every week for about eight weeks but crucially this should be supplemented by daily exercises in the home. This is vital as it brings everyone together in a shared activity. It also contributes to the gradual development of muscle strength and dexterity.

For younger children this might involve something as simple as magnetic fishing games or KerPlunk. Maze or labyrinth games on a computer can also be useful. A family may see benefits in building Lego, in blow football games or in blowing bubbles. These are happy and enjoyable activities and the repetition and practice they encourage will develop confidence and improve self-esteem. The sessions might begin on a one-to-one basis that will help concentration, but this might then move on to small-group work in order to encourage social skills. The particular exercises that are developed can be reinforced in PE lessons.

Shoulder control can be developed through walking on all fours. Pelvic control can be improved through knee walking, cycling and jumping. Throwing and catching a non-threatening object like a beanbag will help hand–eye coordination. Skittles can help. Standing on the spot and touching objects with the foot can assist in many different ways, for example with balance and with midline crossing.

At the end of the programme, the family should be ready to carry on with the exercises to make sure that newly acquired skills are maintained. The family can also develop an interest in different and new types of sport such as rowing or board games such as chess.

All the research seems to indicate that physiotherapy has a beneficial influence and that the improvements made are, in fact, sustained. Children involved in such programmes will show more willingness to try new activities and appear more confident. This is a crucial point: physiotherapy for dyspraxic children is not going to turn them into Olympic athletes but it can have an enormously beneficial influence on all aspects of their development.

8

Apraxia

Developmental verbal dyspraxia, as mentioned in Chapter 1, is also called childhood apraxia of speech. It has all the characteristics of dyspraxia. It affects a child's ability to communicate their thoughts efficiently. It affects that part of human behaviour which distinguishes us from animals, so it goes to the very heart of what it is to be a person. It is not something that can be trivialized.

Those who work in the area, like all who deal with conditions within the dyspraxia spectrum, are keen to point out that apraxia is not a muscle disorder or a cognitive disorder. Once again, it is all about messages from the brain getting scrambled.

As with all forms of dyspraxia the actual causes are unknown. There is speculation of course: a specific small birth injury, or brief oxygen starvation, or a tiny difference in the structure of the speech area of the brain. But no one really knows. The consequences however are obvious.

When you think about it, you will realize just how complex an activity speech is. Anecdotal evidence from my own classroom would suggest that most children don't have too much difficulty in mastering it. But anyone who has difficulty in sequencing physical movement may not only have problems in catching a ball, but also in planning speech movements. Both activities require the sequencing of complicated muscle movements.

Speech is not a deliberately planned activity for most of us. We have things in our heads that we want to say, so we say them. It's automatic. It happens so quickly that it is not always a good thing; often the words pop out before we are ready and we then spend ages putting everything right. But if any part of the process fails to function precisely, then all the linked elements that make up this complex human activity start to unravel. Then we stop communicating effectively. Effective communication requires thought and speech to be tightly integrated. But imagine what it is like if it is not. We might think we are transmitting English, that is the nature of the message we have conceived, but the people around us can only hear Mandarin, which is a pity because they only understand Italian.

So how does speech work? It begins when we have the intention to communicate. There is something that we want to pass on to someone else. So an idea is formed that encompasses what we want to say. Sometimes this happens in an instant, on other occasions it might be a carefully measured and polished statement. In both instances the words must be ordered correctly, in accordance with the appropriate grammatical rules. These words are made up of a specific sequence of sounds. In order to produce the proper sounds there must be precise and highly coordinated movements of the lips, the soft palate, the tongue and the jaw.

Naturally it is the brain that must send out the messages about the exact order and timing of the movements, so that the words are properly articulated. It must also all take place with sufficient strength and muscle tone to ensure that they are accurate sounds which others can interpret with success. It is easy to see how a child with dyspraxic tendencies might find particular difficulty with speech. What is especially interesting is that, because there is nothing wrong with the muscles themselves, the child does not have any problems with non-speech activities performed with the same muscles. They can cough and chew and swallow, but they can't retrieve the plan for making a particular sound. They have put it in the wrong drawer and so it isn't there when they try to find it.

The child knows what they want to say but can't do it at a particular time. The child might not even know how to begin to say the word or the wrong sound might come out. The motor plan to say the word is there all right, but it just can't be found. This means that the child will be able to say the word today quite successfully, but tomorrow they haven't got a hope. Someone has tidied the plan away.

It is certainly no surprise to learn that speech therapists are often the first professionals who are alerted to a dyspraxia problem that might be present in a child they are assessing.

Apraxia and speech therapy are worthy of a book in their own right and it would be doing a lot of professionals a disservice to suggest that these brief words sufficiently describe the contribution they make. It is not the purpose of this book to analyse speech acquisition or to discuss the formation of speech motor plans within the brain.

Bear in mind that speech and language disorders are the number one disability in children. The cause of many of these problems could be ascribed to dyspraxia or to elements of the condition, for there is, as we have seen, a considerable overlap, or co-morbidity, between many associated impairments. A child with dyspraxia might also carry with them aspects from other conditions like ADHD or dyslexia or even Tourette's syndrome. This suggests to some that all these conditions are linked through the same sort of brain dysfunction.

This co-morbidity, however, can be a problem. It could mean that the accompanying condition is the one that receives treatment and the child may not then receive the therapies that would help to address the communication impairment. If it continues undiagnosed, or the problems continue to be attributed to other things, then their chances of future success in communication could be compromised. A residual outcome of these disorders is the likelihood of developing learning disorders. It is obvious really, how can you demonstrate what you have learned if you can't communicate it? How can you process knowledge when that knowledge is presented through the medium of language? Yet these children may well have an understanding of the structure of language that will be far superior to their production of language.

Often they will have a limited speech-sound repertoire. They will have very few sounds that they can access successfully, so they might use a simple syllable like 'da' to stand for almost anything. As their speech develops their main characteristic will be inconsistency.

The letter 'l' might be fine until it follows a 'p', so 'pull' will be accurate but 'plum' will become 'pyum'.

The longer a phrase the worse the accuracy in speech. And, of course, they will not grow out of it without intervention. Their speech will improve as they mature but it will still be littered with errors and prove difficult to understand. They might need therapy for at least two years, perhaps longer, but they can most definitely improve.

There is a range of therapies which can be employed. These can involve repetitive songs and games. Sign language can provide the child with a means of showing others what they want and what they know. Communicating through pictures can also be valuable. A speech therapist will tell you that the approach must be frequent and intensive. However, as with all aspects of dyspraxia, there is no quick fix. It is not a condition that can be neatly parcelled up and then sorted out. Nevertheless, once the child has made himself understood then he will want to stop using any alternative methods because spoken language is so much easier and so much more flexible. He will therefore support efforts to achieve improvement.

Apraxia can act as a useful indication of the frustrations that a child with dyspraxia might feel. Things are inside their head that just won't come out. They will want to communicate but might find it increasingly difficult. Don't ever forget that dyspraxic children are often very bright. The correct word they are seeking may be filed away somewhere in their brain where it isn't readily accessible. We all know what this is like. We've all found ourselves unable to remember a name. 'It's on the tip of my tongue,' we will say. Imagine feeling like this all the time, with thoughts racing around your head but being unable to pin any of them down effectively.

When we write, we project what is inside our heads to the rest of the world. I am projecting what is inside my head to you, wherever you are, through my writing. If I don't do it properly then I cannot hope to make you understand what is inside my head, and I cannot then hope to influence what is happening inside your own head. It is the same when we are talking. Others draw conclusions from our abilities to project our thoughts with clarity. If you are not very good at it then you are quickly judged. Incoherent speech? Incoherent mind.

If the real world is frustrating and unsympathetic because it doesn't seem to understand you, then a lack of confidence is inevitable. Then it may be easier to retreat into an interior world which doesn't need to be projected and where everything is obvious and simple. There are many ways in which dyspraxic children need to be helped but a focus upon successful communication, especially verbal communication, is vital. An inability to communicate easily impacts on both social interaction and language development. There are other consequences too.

If it is the muscles in the mouth that are preventing clear speech, it is possible that chewing will be difficult too. Cutlery could be tricky. And being a 'messy eater' can mean not being invited to parties and soon becoming the victim of unpleasant comments. Siblings may be embarrassed to bring their friends home. This can build resentment. As you can see, there is a social dimension to having dyspraxia.

As you can see, the speech therapist should become an important ally. They have a crucial part to play.

9

How to Teach a Child with Dyspraxia

There is no big secret, no special formula. Good teaching that is structured and focused works for dyspraxic children just as much as it does for everyone else. So be sure to stick to your principles and you won't go far wrong. But of course there are particular features of dyspraxia that you need to note carefully. These may help to explain the ways in which a dyspraxic child can respond. Before we examine the specific issues that a child might present at the different stages of their school career, there are some general points that we need to consider.

It will certainly help if you do your research and familiarize yourself with the condition. You will achieve a deeper understanding and you will be better placed to discuss the child with their parents and offer informed advice. A well-informed teacher, especially in the early years, can provide a great deal of assistance. By reading this book you have already shown a willingness to enhance your knowledge and to be sensitive to their needs. Many of the difficulties you encounter with an individual child will make more sense if you have a context in which to put the information. With this understanding, you can work out the best way of teaching the child and maximizing achievement.

Dyspraxia

In the frantic activity that makes up a normal day in school it is all too easy to forget what you should remember, and you may find yourself condemning a dyspraxic child for things that they have no control over. If they forget things then it isn't always their fault. An inability to recall stored information is a difficulty in the processes of storing rather than of memory and is certainly not a sign of laziness. Remember how those messages are being re-routed along twisting suburban lines behind a slow engine. The child probably wants to learn things just as much as the next but for them learning takes 20 times the normal effort. This is the case whether the child has to learn where the pencils are kept, where the toilets are or to remember the details of Thomas Hardy's poetry. In fact, any information learned might not be reliably recalled. It could get lost in transit for neurological reasons as we have seen – an idea suddenly shunted into weedy sidings away from the main line. The child shouldn't be blamed for this.

Here are some suggestions for teaching a dyspraxic child.

♦ First of all, any teacher needs to ensure that instructions are broken down and simplified. It is important to maintain eye contact when giving instructions to an individual dyspraxic child. This will help them to concentrate.

♦ Explain things in a simple uncomplicated way. Make sure your instructions remain constant and unchanged.

♦ Remember, almost everything can be broken down into a staged process with a logical sequence. It is one of the things that teachers are good at and all children in a class can benefit from this approach, whether dyspraxic or not.

♦ In these circumstances patience is a virtue. Be prepared to repeat yourself calmly and frequently.

♦ With younger children in particular it can be helpful to repeat things gently, leading and prompting the memory until previous learning can be recalled. Just as music can prompt forgotten ideas and experiences in all of us, so the memory can be prompted through a rhythmical, phonological approach to issues such as reading, writing and maths. Sing or chant or clap – but link it to a particular concept.

♦ Ensure that you communicate your expectations clearly and concisely. Ask questions to ensure they know what to do. Ask them to repeat the task to you before they begin.

♦ Offer encouragement and keep reminding the class of the task and the sequence.

♦ It is always helpful to establish a predictable routine and firm guidelines. Sudden changes in routine can cause major problems for a child with dyspraxia.

♦ Simplify choices. We are all surrounded by too many choices that we don't need. A dyspraxic child is perhaps less able to deal with them than most. In these circumstances choice doesn't bring freedom, it brings confusion. So why offer six different essay titles? Is anyone really disadvantaged if they only have two?

Dyspraxia

♦ Ensure that the child knows where they are in the overall shape of the lesson and how much time they have left. Give them clear time checks, for example 'There are ten minutes to go, so start bringing this section to a close'. Make sure there is a clock visible. This is a very important technique to acquire for examinations.

♦ A dyspraxic child might need additional time to complete a task satisfactorily.

♦ Stay alert to the child's needs. They may find it difficult to wait for adult attention, so be ready to seize the moment.

♦ Try to minimize distractions. A child with dyspraxia may be very distractable so a simplified classroom will help. Keep screens and boards free of unnecessary information as an aid to concentration. This will encourage focus.

♦ Sitting at the front will help concentration by reducing intrusive distractions.

♦ Remember that they are emotionally fragile. They might be unable to deal with disapproval or criticism within the context intended. A careless or casual word could provoke a disproportionate response. Try to stay calm and learn to manage your own feelings of guilt when an unguarded word leaves them devastated.

As a teacher you will know that reading, writing and maths all require a great deal of planning and organization. It is possible therefore that the real nature of any difficulties may not show up properly until the demands of the classroom become more structured, when you will see a child who is unable to retain learning consistently. You will see the disruption caused by problems such as handwriting, reading and following instructions, which may obscure the child's intellectual potential.

What is most frustrating is the inconsistency that comes with dyspraxia. What a child knows today they may not know tomorrow. The plan needed to perform a task could disappear suddenly. They may become less articulate when excited or upset. Long stories or explanations can't be sustained and there might be constant repetitions of statements and questions as the child fights to maintain concentration and fix information in their head. And from many of these issues there is no escape.

Taking a dyspraxic child away from school on a visit could be especially challenging for a teacher, who would have to confront all the difficulties normally contained within the family. Residential experiences are today increasingly popular at all levels. In these circumstances it would be wise to establish a dialogue with parents at an early stage. Exchange visits where the child stays with the family of another student overseas can be quite stressful. However, as long as the placements are chosen properly and the hosts fully informed, there is no reason why they should be excluded from the benefits that there are in living abroad with another family.

We can start now to look at the different stages of schooling. A lot of the advice in the following chapters is transferable from one stage to another. A child's requirements don't necessarily change when they move from one school to another. So it may be that

Dyspraxia

ideas that can help are outside the age range of particular concern. A child at any age could still have all the problems presented by a pre-school child with little or no improvement. The emphasis throughout must be on good teaching that supports children and their learning.

At all stages of education your responsibility is to use your knowledge to support parents. It is likely that their experience and understanding of the condition will be limited. Their child's difficulties might have come as a complete shock to them, but you will have met more than one dyspraxic. You will have experience to draw upon and you will be able to offer reassurance and bring much-needed knowledge and strategies.

You will act as a mediator between the child and their family and an apparently hostile world. I know that the child will appreciate your attention and the space that you give them. Just imagine how it might feel for a child who may have been victimized or rejected to find an important and significant adult who is prepared to give them unquestioned attention before it is given to anyone else. That's what you need to show as a teacher: sensitivity and a commitment to rescuing a child's self-esteem.

We are talking about active teaching here. The desire and the awareness to do what is right. But of course there is also a need for active parenting. They must understand that their special child can't be abandoned to a life on the streets and a microwave pizza for tea. No child should experience this, but a dyspraxic child demands active support and structured help. Parents need to understand this. They need to get informed and this is where you can help, for they have so much information to take in.

But it is not all bad news. The whole family can benefit too. A family with a child with any kind of disability can be a handicapped family. The family needs to deal with the issues it faces as a unit. All members can benefit from a deliberately chosen and enhanced diet for example (for more about this see Chapter 17). The kind of games and activities that help dyspraxics could become a shared family experience. It could be argued that it might alienate a sibling who feels ignored in the face of these special needs but let's be positive, it will certainly have the effect of broadening their perspective, of showing them that we are not all the same, that there are significant differences between us all, that we all have abilities as well as inabilities. Let's celebrate the differences between our children. Let's emphasize everyone's worth and stress the unique contribution that they can make. Let's use dyspraxia to bind the family together.

10

Dyspraxia in Pre-school and Nursery

All teachers – at whatever stage – can make a great deal of difference to the development of dyspraxic children through their understanding and patience and through a commitment to preserving and boosting self-esteem. Where teachers of the pre-school child are especially valuable, in nurseries and playgroups for example, is in giving support to parents who may be coming to terms with a recent diagnosis or, more likely, trying to understand why their lovely child is somehow different. Teachers of this age group need to have readily available practical strategies for support, both for children and their parents.

You really will be in the front line in managing the condition and the parents. In playgroup or nursery, as with all children, vital foundations are laid, for better a for worse. If basic skills are not successfully established, then everything in the future could be compromised. Problems that become obviously apparent later on are first seen here to a greater or lesser extent.

An observant teacher or professional might look at a child and begin to form a picture. They will be slowly accumulating evidence. They should register concerns when they see a child

Dyspraxia

- who is less inclined to participate in play
- who is less active than others
- who avoids large play equipment
- who is more passive, more anxious
- who has speech problems, perhaps caused by poor control over the small muscles in the mouth.

A child's reputation may already start to coalesce as that of an outsider, slightly beyond the fringe of interaction and activity.

At this stage they are not usually labelled or ostracized. Children at this stage will generally accept others for what they are, but the process of isolation may have started. Dyspraxics learn very quickly that there are things they find harder to do than others and even at this young age they will not want to be different from their friends, but they have little choice and their different responses to the everyday world are soon apparent.

- Some dyspraxic children are hypersensitive to certain stimuli. They might have an aversion to bright lights or loud noises. You can notice this on occasions like Bonfire Night or at Christmas. Such an aversion could become discernible if the child is involved in a play or a performance, especially when they are older. They could be very uncomfortable under bright lights. This will become a common theme for dyspraxics. Wanting to be involved in something and their body stopping it from happening.

♦ There could be an oversensitivity to certain textures like the labels on clothes or to wool. They could take particular objection to hair combing or nail cutting.

♦ They may appear touch-sensitive and shy away from any sort of contact. They might be irritable when nudged, for example.

♦ The child may seem accident-prone, more clumsy than most, lacking in basic coordination. They may have poor stability when moving.

♦ They may look awkward when running, walking or even standing still. Can they actually stand still? And how do they stand? With feet splayed out? Can they stand on one leg? They could have floppy limbs caused by poor muscle control around a particular joint. All these things are significant features.

♦ They could be very messy or untidy eaters. They could in fact have difficulty in coordinating the sequence of chewing then swallowing.

♦ They could be slow in learning new games and their rules.

♦ A skill mastered today can be forgotten tomorrow.

♦ They might have no concept at all of position, such as behind, in front, on, etc.

♦ You may find that they have an astonishing memory in one particular area. They may be able, for example, to identify any make of car they see with uncanny accuracy from a minimum of information. However, they may have a poor memory for things that they hear.

Dyspraxia

♦ Making choices could be extremely difficult.

♦ They might not be able to follow simple instructions in the correct sequence.

The child could be having problems making sense of a world that seems to be flying past at high speed, never slowing down long enough for them to get a grip on things.

It is essential that teachers plan a range of strategies in the classroom so that these children can demonstrate the skills and knowledge they possess. What is clear is that children as young as six evaluate themselves globally. In other words, they don't think, 'I'm no good at writing or drawing,' they think, 'I'm no good at all!' This has to be prevented at all costs.

Teachers, knowing the concentration and effort a dyspraxic child has to show, must respond to genuine examples of progress and offer immediate praise so that the children are encouraged to continue with their efforts, rather than give up.

It is not just the children who find this a difficult time. It is tough for parents too. They will want the best for their child and may sense that something is not quite right. They have the suspicion but not the name. If a diagnosis has not yet been made then they may acquire a reputation as being over-anxious parents among those who do not understand the condition. This could certainly affect the way that they are seen by some schools. Professionals should always ask themselves why parents have concerns. Are they legitimate? Are they justified?

You need to listen to their observations because they know far more about their own child than anyone else.

Never dismiss them out of hand. Never assume the parents don't know what they are talking about.

It could be a very frustrating time for parents, trying to convince a doctor that something is wrong. It is not unknown for parents to be seen as fussy or troublesome. They might need someone to take their concerns seriously and to listen. It is a very important time, for it might be when the first interventions and strategies begin. Parents might need you to reassure them that their child's problems with the labels on clothes is not too alarming or indeed unique.

Parents will want to know the answers to many questions and they will also want to find out what they can do to make things better for the child that they love. A simple series of graded exercises to be carried out either at school or in the home could be proposed. An example could be walking between two lines about a foot apart. This will help coordination and could be part of a game for everyone, not just a child with dyspraxic tendencies. Then you could move on to riding a scooter between the lines. This can take on a more imaginative dimension if this path is imagined as the route to a special place or the route to a reward.

There are lots of things that a teacher of the youngest dyspraxics can do which will provide solid foundations for future progress.

♦ Simple activities that can link school and home have a big impact. Enjoyable activities that the child wants to do really make a difference. So you should encourage parents and carers to use any poems or songs that have actions such as Simon Says. This helps copying, listening skills and body awareness.

Adults need to be sympathetic with the speed of the instructions they give, perhaps making a significant pause so that the dyspraxic child has extra time to prepare for what they are required to do.

♦ Other games like Incy Wincy Spider, Heads, Shoulders, Knees and Toes, or In a Cottage in a Wood are also useful. They are very good for developing finger dexterity and fitting the speed of the actions to the speed of the song as well as for body awareness.

♦ Another good game is Pass the Parcel. This game helps laterality by promoting an awareness of passing to the side and then promotes fine motor skills when the parcel has to be unwrapped. The children can sit and push the parcel round with their feet as a variation. This is difficult, but fun for a brief spell.

♦ Another useful game is something called Angels in the Snow. Children lie flat on the floor on their backs and then sweep their arms and legs wide, then together at the same time. Next they can sweep one arm and leg on the same side, then the opposite side, wide and together. The children can then lie on their backs in a circle, with their fingertips touching to make an angel design. As the teacher says 'Swish', the children in unison move their arms and legs to open and close the star. It could be a good thing to video for the children to see the consequences of their actions and how cooperation and coordination can be creative processes. It is also a very good way of helping children feel where the backs of all their body parts are. Warn parents that it is going to happen though: it is always good to prevent a laundry crisis.

♦ A teacher should emphasize the fantasy and emotional elements of the children's play. This will encourage them to do more, since they will then concentrate upon the artificial world and its implications rather than the mechanics of performance.

♦ Give children plenty of warning that they are expected to transfer from one activity to another. Dyspraxic children find these transitions difficult to organize.

♦ Children respond best in a routine which is predictable and structured.

♦ It is believed that you can enhance body awareness by providing some resistance to a child's movements. If they are pushing a reasonably heavy pram or trolley then they will be more aware of what they need to do because their movements will be slowed down. In the same way, walking up a ramp or even up steps can be more helpful than walking along the flat.

♦ Games that include space or direction words can be very valuable, for example 'Go under your partner's legs or climb through the barrel', 'Go onto the top of the box then jump down and come back to the start.' By doing this you are reinforcing a sense of direction and of order.

♦ Ask the child to help you build an obstacle course to develop these skills. The planning and the building will help organizational abilities and promote self-confidence. It will help them to learn how to judge distances and examine consequences. The obstacle course itself will help to develop motor abilities.

♦ You can then ask questions as they negotiate the circuits, for example 'You are very good at climbing. Now tell me, how are you going to get down?'

♦ Engage, if you can, with the child's play. Join in with their activities without asking questions and without demands. They will benefit from having to direct your part in it through clear instructions. They will see the consequences of the things they suggest.

♦ Following on from the last point, you may then expand upon the themes established by the child in related activities. This will enable the child to build upon their play and extend it, rather than return always to the familiar theme.

♦ Always allow for repetition and practice. They will need this time to firm up the skills they are trying to acquire.

Much of what you do will provide a secure foundation for what will happen later in the child's school career. You can put in place simple things that will have a huge influence later on. For example, you can begin to improve their quality of movement and develop greater confidence in spatial awareness. You will be helping their brains to refine and improve the connections that need to be made.

A teacher at this early stage can make a significant contribution to improvements in movement. It is a long, slow process, but slight improvements will eventually combine to produce noticeable benefits. The activities chosen must be simple enough to allow the child to succeed, but structured to bring about both progress and understanding. The child needs to know how the improvement was achieved. It is important that children recognize what they did. They must understand how their movements were refined to allow them to be successful. If this happens, there is more chance that the child will be able to transfer or at least adapt these movements effectively in different environments.

Some of the things that work are really simple and children enjoy them because success is easily measured and perceived. Jumping over a line stretched between cones and placed at different heights can be a good way to start. You can then include movement activities in an obstacle course. Using different height levels and spacings that require readjustment and a change in direction is effective as the child has to distribute their body weight in different ways as well as adjust the speed and effort they must put into a specific action or movement.

Expressive movement can be a very useful activity. It not only aids the development of gross motor skills, particularly as the child moves from one action to another, but it also encourages children to distinguish between the different qualities and characteristics of the actions, thus making a valuable contribution to the development of their vocabulary.

♦ You can start with walking, which can move on to creeping or sauntering or prowling or stalking.

Dyspraxia

◆ Running can become dashing, darting, rushing, zipping.

◆ Jumping can move into bounding, exploding, popping or leaping.

◆ On-the-spot activities can be developed such as pointing, turning, twisting, stretching, sinking or growing.

◆ You can ask the class to freeze or to wait or pause.

Don't forget though that dyspraxic children find it difficult to stand still, so don't ask them to sustain it for too long. If the teacher or the children themselves select one word from each type of action here, they can be ordered into an expressive movement phrase, for example 'Creep and freeze, bound and explode!' This sequence includes contrasts in speed and distance. Movements on the spot need to be included to give the children time to prepare for the next action. All children and especially dyspraxic children, who are characteristically underachievers in these areas, will love giving instructions that the whole class must follow.

Structured movements like these are really important learning activities. They require control and planning. There might be balance problems as the child manages the transitions but they will not be alone in experiencing these. And the repetition of such activities will have significant beneficial effects.

Perhaps the most important thing you will have to deal with is the parents themselves. Their most obvious question will be whether their child will ever grow out of their dyspraxia. Your professional responsibility is to be honest: they will probably not grow out of it. What might happen though is that over time they will adapt their behaviour to accommodate the difficulties they have. They will learn to live with them and to manage them, if they get the right help. Once an awareness of their difficulties is raised then proper interventions may begin so as a teacher you must not feel inhibited. The earlier the process is started, the better it is for everyone.

11

Dyspraxia in Primary School

What is it that the parents of dyspraxic children want when they send their child to primary school? They want a school with a warm and welcoming atmosphere, a caring institution, friendly and approachable staff.

These are things that every parent wants. But then their list shows a fundamental difference. What they then say is that they want a school with a uniform that has no ties, no laces and no buttons.

When you deal with dyspraxic children, you are dealing with children who are different and as they grow older those differences can worry parents more. As they approach the time to leave primary school and to move on, they will ask whether their child can cope with the way in which their life is about to change.

Arriving in primary school itself is a particularly serious moment of change. The familiarity of home is replaced by the uncertainties of school. There are new, unfamiliar people; there is new furniture to bump into. It can be a very unsettling experience. A well-informed and sensitive teacher can make a big difference.

Teachers should never underestimate the importance of their job and in this section we will look at the influence the teacher can have and the strategies that can be adopted to support the dyspraxic children in their care in the crucial primary years.

The child may have managed to avoid certain activities in playgroup or nursery as a way of hiding their difficulties. However, in primary school the curriculum becomes more structured and formal and they will have to confront their problems. They will have to deal with large amounts of new and confusing information and more specific physical demands. Certainly the gaps between children will widen, and conclusions will be drawn about those who can't carry out particular activities with confidence, such as catching a ball, dressing, eating and other domestic tasks.

The child may have significant issues to face – such as using the toilet efficiently, managing clothing, playing with other children, adjusting to a new classroom. After all, it is a busy and noisy place, in the middle of which the dyspraxic child is supposed to sit still. They may, for example, find themselves sitting with their back to the teacher for part of a lesson. They will have to maintain attention while dodging backwards and forwards to follow the focus of the topic. This could be very difficult.

They are quite likely to have poor visual and auditory tracking. Visual tracking affects competences like copying from the board into a book on a flat desk just as much as it affects following the flight path of a ball. It is almost inevitable that they will lose their place in the same way that the ball is likely to hit them before they are ready for it.

Auditory tracking can mean difficulty in listening to and in following instructions, especially if the teacher moves around into different parts of the room while they are speaking. It is also clear that children with dyspraxic difficulties can be seen copying the reactions of others when they receive instructions rather than initiating actions. This is because there is obviously a significant delay in the processing of the information. Being dyspraxic is hard work, you must be constantly aware of what others are doing so that you don't get left behind and teased.

The move to the primary school could be a very tiring time, for the school day will be longer, with different rules and requirements. A teacher may quickly form the impression that a child has significant levels of immaturity in a number of areas, for example in writing and drawing. What may trouble them most of all could be an inability to concentrate that will definitely have an impact on attainment. But a teacher isn't powerless: always remember, there are things that you can do that will make a difference.

At home, the family manages problem situations, but in primary school the same activities need to be managed alone – like getting changed or putting a coat on – for the child will, naturally, be spending a significant time away from their parents.

This is important to note, and before looking at learning issues in the classroom, a primary teacher will have to consider a number of significant domestic issues so that the real business of school can take place. In order to do this, teachers and other classroom workers need to have an understanding of these issues so that they can go on to offer advice and solutions to parents. Here are some useful points:

Dyspraxia

- Parents could be advised to label clothes clearly.

- Suggest that parents choose a school bag with roomy and separate pockets, then separate out personal items, like dinner, into one pocket and school things, like a pencil case, into another. Always put them in the same place. This will help packing and checking if things have their own special place. A diagonal strap distributes weight more evenly and helps children who have balancing difficulties.

- They should look for Velcro fastenings on shoes.

- Elasticated waists on shorts and trousers can be helpful. Pleated trousers make it easier to distinguish the front from the back.

- PE kit could be worn under normal school clothing in order to minimize difficulties.

- Personal hygiene could be a problem. An electric toothbrush will help to sort out one area at least.

- A sensitive teacher will also watch closely and lend discreet assistance when necessary, to other children as well as dyspraxics, in order to minimize any embarrassment in dealing with personal issues.

- Eating in school could be a real problem. Cutlery may still be difficult to master and a child could become particularly self-conscious, so perhaps sandwiches are a better practical alternative. It would be better to wrap them in foil rather than use clingfilm which can often defeat the best of us. Firm sandwich fillings like cheese are easier to handle than sloppy ones. Make sure that biscuits can be unwrapped easily.

♦ Suggest that parents provide drinks which don't need pouring. Boxes of juice with a straw are a simple solution, just so long as the child does not squeeze the box against their body, thus spraying juice everywhere.

I am afraid to say that if we have problems getting the food in at one end then we can have just as many with excreta at the other. The child may not leave itself enough time to get to the toilet. They may not recognize the signals soon enough so that by the time they get there they might be in a bit of a rush. If you add on the tricky business of getting trousers up and down then you will see that the potential for accidents is extensive.

The processes involved in wiping the bottom might be difficult to coordinate. So the opportunities for embarrassment are huge and as a result a child might try to avoid the experience altogether. One of the results can be constipation. You might want to discuss with parents the idea of establishing a regular toileting regime. Going to the toilet at the same time every day, perhaps before school, could definitely help. Elasticated waistbands should be recommended and the school should have a ready supply of wet wipes. It may be that the muscles in the bladder will be less efficient and toilet training could be insecure and with frequent accidents, especially in times of stress. Children may forget to go or get little warning and so teachers have to allow immediate access to toilets.

All of these public difficulties and occasional failings will have a hugely negative impact on the child's self-esteem if, as seems likely, their reputation is undermined. Vigilance is required to prevent this happening.

The routine involved in visiting the toilet should be reinforced at regular intervals with emphasis placed upon hygiene. The whole class will benefit from this anyway.

There are other symptoms of control that will also have an impact on learning. The obvious factors that will hinder achievement in school are problems with coordination and manipulation. There are, however, things that a teacher can do. You don't have to accept things as they are. You can do things that really will make things better. And, as small improvements accumulate through repeated practice, then gradually significant progress will be noted.

What the teacher can do to help

Writing

A dyspraxic child may not have developed an appropriate tripod grip for writing. Their grip might weaken quickly or they may apply too much pressure in order to maintain control. Handwriting can thus appear uneven and crude. It might not be possible to write along a line or to keep words separate. Letter formation might not be consistent and writing at the top of the page could be better than that at the bottom. The following points may help to improve a child's writing:

♦ Experiment and try to find a pen that the child finds easy to hold. There are lots of pens around these days – with foam grips or with textured barrels for example. Triangular-shaped pens are sometimes a successful solution.

♦ If written work is sometimes too untidy then allow the use of a pencil, just as long as the child does not repeatedly press down too hard and so snap the lead. Mistakes can be erased easily and the finished product will look more acceptable to the child.

♦ Inclined boards for reading and writing can make an enormous difference. These can be improvised simply if funds are short. They help to ease visual tracking from the board or screen to the exercise book. They also ease pressure on the wrist during writing. An inclined board will also help reading because the eyes are less likely to jump over letters since the angle helps to achieve focus.

♦ Fix paper or books to the boards with masking tape if necessary. This ensures that the book does not wobble and helps handwriting.

♦ Make sure that overhead lights don't glare or reflect directly on the child's work. This makes visual difficulties worse.

♦ Experiment by playing Mozart in class as an aid to concentration.

♦ Of course, a computer can help to make work presentable and indistinguishable from the work of anyone else. Computer skills are important for the future anyway.

Dyspraxia

♦ A child still needs to acquire some facility in hand-writing; however difficult it is, it can't be replaced entirely. Repetitive exercises on letter formation can be employed as a means of slowly improving hand-writing, but writing out a favourite poem or piece from a story can be more fun and reinforces the emphasis on learning.

♦ Be careful if you need to ask for untidy work to be done again. The child will know that repetition usually means that something was wrong in the first place. It is better to talk about 'redrafting' and 'final copies'. Without such sensitivity, the child's sense of failure could be continually confirmed, switching them off from education entirely.

♦ The oral work of dyspraxic children can often be of a much higher standard than their written work. This is because human development is cephalocaudal, which means that it progresses from head to toe, and proximodistal, which means from the centre of the body out to the peripheries. As a result, control of the extremities like hands and feet is the last thing to be developed. This is why ideas will be inside the head but will struggle to drop off the end of the fingers – they have such a long way to go. To allow children like these to be successful, teachers could consider alternative strategies. Oral storytelling for story writing or having the children tape-record their stories so that they can be written a few sentences at a time can be useful assessment approaches. They can also demonstrate their knowledge more easily in discussions and other oral situations that can be effectively assessed and moderated.

Music

Music has an important part to play. It stresses a sense of order and sequence. However, learning to play the recorder, that integral part of the primary experience, can be difficult if you don't have reliable fine control of the fingers. Perhaps the drums would be a better alternative. Repeating patterns and structures in increasingly complex forms could be very beneficial. It is a good and creative way of easing frustrations too.

Songs and word games like 'I went to market' can be very successful as a way of teaching memory and sequence. Children enjoy it and want to be part of the fun and this will encourage concentration and involvement.

A simple task like striking the triangle or a xylophone at the right moment during a performance could do a huge amount for self-esteem and be important in encouraging teamwork. It is an act of inclusion for children who can be frequently excluded by their peers.

Dance

Dance can have a very important part to play, particularly ensemble work. It provides a forum in which to learn about and develop structured movement. When children move together and then apart in a planned way they develop an awareness of the movements of others and have to adjust their timing and use of space to be part of the overall design.

One idea is for four children to dance together, using movements practised in pairs, adjusting their use of space and so composing a group dance. This could include parts where everyone moves together and actions are performed in sequence. Again, awareness of other children, memorizing the short dance and retaining the quality of the chosen movements provides an enjoyable challenge. Of course, remembering what comes next helps planning and sequencing.

The children should be encouraged to select actions that allow them to show contrasts, for these blend easily and very satisfyingly into a rhythmical dance.

Setting the dance to words, for example 'turn and hold, turn and hold, jump away, jump away, crumple and freeze', and repeating the words as the dance progresses, gives time for a rhythm to develop. The repetition allows children to remember what it is they should be doing. If some children find turning difficult, they can take their time on the 'hold' part so that their balance is re-established ready for the next movement.

While one group is working, other children in the class who are watching can try to guess the words the dancers are demonstrating if this is a vocabulary exercise. Others could accompany the dance with percussion. In this way everyone is able to participate and to learn words along with their different shades of meaning as well as learning about the dance.

Scissors and hand control

Scissors might be very hard to use. Holding the paper in one hand and then making the correct open and close movements could be almost impossible. Spring-assisted scissors could reduce coordination difficulties. Starting with stiffer paper could help. Cutting squares or rectangles from a long strip is a way of developing skills. It is, however, going to be a long, hard struggle.

There are other activities that can be employed to support improvement in hand control.

Winding a lace round a bobbin is very difficult and is a real test of fine motor skill. All sorts of threading activities can be very beneficial and there are many commercial variants of this activity that parents can also get involved in to help skills to grow. A nail pattern hammered into wood in the form of a spider's web allows children to hold with one hand and wind wool with the other. This helps coordination and shows how actions can have creative and unexpected outcomes.

Lego can also help manipulation. Building with bricks helps planning and sequencing. Hand exercises or the making of shapes with clay or plasticine can warm up the muscles before activities such as writing begin. Screwing loose plastic nuts and bolts together is another obvious activity that helps coordination.

Rulers and other equipment

Using a ruler can be awkward since it requires the child to hold it down with one hand and to draw with the other. A metal 'safety ruler' with a groove stamped into it, or one with a raised handle or ridge might help. You can make handles for smaller pieces of mathematical equipment with lumps of Blu-Tack. A compass is another tool that is difficult to master. A blob of Blu-Tack into which the point can be placed aids stability and accuracy.

Sequencing

When you consider how the brain might be having difficulty remembering certain actions, it will be no surprise to learn that sequencing could be a problem.

You can help by using picture stories and asking the child to put them in the right order.

It is very useful for dyspraxic children to have lots of estimating games in the classroom: for example, How many long steps will you need to place the ball in the box? Which kind of ball will you choose if you are going to bounce a ball over the box? The children can estimate and then try it out! The skills in making judgements are important because they involve making decisions and assessing the consequences of any actions.

Another good way to start is with something like Sweets in the Jar. The child must guess the number of sweets or cubes in a jar. They will need to unscrew the lid, empty them out, count them and then fill the jar again. Holding the jar with one hand and unscrewing the lid is very difficult for a dyspraxic child but it is important that it is practised. At first the children will clamp the jar into their bodies for extra support but with practice they should eventually be able to hold it on the table to unscrew the lid.

Classroom management

♦ One of the most important things that a primary teacher can do to help is to make sure that the dyspraxic child sits facing the teacher as much as possible, as maintaining eye contact can be an important aid to concentration.

♦ Simplify the environment too if you can. Don't provide too many auditory or visual distractions.

♦ Instructions might need to be broken down into smaller and easily digestible steps. Gently repeat things and lead the memory until previous learning can be recalled. Don't give them too many choices as this will act merely to confuse.

♦ The teacher should ensure that all work is presented in short steps or stages and that the child is asked to repeat the instructions given to reinforce understanding. It will sometimes be beneficial to use worksheets and exercises allowing for short and structured responses in order to reduce the amount of handwriting required.

♦ Your expectations should be communicated clearly and concisely, and, while you must not employ extreme or false praise, because in the end we all learn to see through this, ensure that you don't knock their self-esteem with unguarded comments.

♦ Keep an eye on them. They will find it very difficult to wait for adult attention because it will be hard to keep a grip on the ideas or questions they wish to express.

♦ The child will need a predictable routine since sudden changes can be particularly unsettling.

♦ Select grouping arrangements with care, and natu-rally don't label the dyspraxic child as slow just because their writing is weak. They have other valuable intellectual strengths which mean that they can contribute in an effective way in group situations. This can be an important way of improving self-esteem and the way they are seen by their peers.

◆ Remember, group work can build bridges between children if the groups are selected sensitively.

◆ Classroom support assistants can achieve a great deal with dyspraxic children if they are deployed effectively. They can work on particular exercises targeted to make a positive impact. You will always find that dyspraxic children enjoy individual attention and can thrive in situations where they are not competing with their peers. It is compensation for playground neglect. They crave acceptance and enjoy responsibility. Being with their teacher or other adults gives them time when they can find both these things. Additional adults in the classroom can help the busy teacher achieve these sorts of objectives, which would otherwise be very difficult to schedule.

◆ The observant teacher will see other problems that will be a cause for special concern. Social skills might be poor and interaction with others clumsy or uncertain. In many ways, this might trouble parents much more than anything else at this stage. They will begin to fear what the future might hold for a child who is finding making and maintaining relationships a serious challenge.

It should be quite clear by now that a dyspraxic child lives with lots of frustrations, and sometimes that frustration boils over. It shouldn't be a surprise. The child may become suddenly aggressive or disruptive or far too easily moved to tears. There may be a real sense of anger because the child will want to do better but is aware that something intangible is interfering with achievement.

It is also very possible that the child can become a victim of bullying. As a boy he will be regarded as immature. He will be excluded from games and spend a lot of time on his own. He will walk round the edge of the playground rather than be active in the middle. He may seek the company of either younger children or of adults who will accept him more readily. It doesn't take long for a reputation to be formed within a peer group. Suddenly they are someone who isn't quite the same as everyone else. To a child at this stage, conformity is everything. And as friendships form and coalesce, suddenly a child can become a loner, generally because of the things they can't do. These issues are explored in more detail in 'The emotional minefield' section (pp. 107–10).

You may observe these things. And it is important that you share your observations with colleagues and other professionals. You need to liaise closely with your informed Special Educational Needs Coordinator (SENCO). The more efficiently the information is passed around between colleagues, the more successful an experience school will become.

You must also stay in touch with parents. They will probably be very pleased that someone can confirm their own doubts and concerns. This might indeed be the first stage of more formal assessments. You can also refer parents to relevant publications (see Resources) which could be very reassuring and productive.

Dyspraxia

All children find primary school very tiring. For the child with dyspraxia the problems are magnified, completing simple actions will require even greater concentration and focus. A teacher needs to be aware that quieter periods of relaxation are vital if they are to help the child manage the amount of information that is in danger of swamping them on a daily basis.

Of course, as the child progresses through the school, their ability to deal with different situations will improve. A dyspraxic child isn't fixed forever within an unresponsive body. They do change, they do develop naturally, though perhaps at a slower rate. The remedial exercises suggested should eventually have an impact. So the child will change, their confidence in some situations will improve, their concentration and focus will develop. It is just a longer process. Sadly, sometimes that process extends beyond the traditional school-leaving age.

Primary school teaching does become more formal and separates into different subjects with different requirements. It is all part of the inevitable process that feeds through into the timetabled structure of secondary school. This formality often brings with it greater assessment, both internal and external.

Schools need to have the statementing process well in place by this stage. This might guarantee the child who is pressured for time, due to organizational issues, more space in which to show their real abilities. This will not be appropriate for all dyspraxics, but where in the teacher's estimation it will be helpful, children need to be encouraged to accept that there is no shame in taking extra time. They are entitled to it.

There is a fundamental point here. With equal opportunities legislation, discrimination laws and accessibility legislation, it is vital that all education institutions recognize and support any student with dyspraxia just as with all other conditions, whether they are visible difficulties or hidden ones.

Homework

This is a big issue. Schools at all levels pride themselves on their wide-ranging and robust homework policy. It is a means by which they promote themselves. They ask others to make judgements about them on the basis of homework. They like to think that it shows they are a no-nonsense institution devoted to learning and academic achievement. Whether this is accurate or not, homework does give the dyspraxic child some difficulties.

For a start they may have to concentrate and work much harder than the other pupils in the class. This means they may be very tired by the time they get home. At this point they are expected to do more of what they found difficult in the first place. It is a difficult issue because they don't want to be singled out by not doing homework, but at the same time they could feel totally overwhelmed.

Their greatest need is for organization, and both home and school can help here.

♦ A homework diary needs to be kept.

♦ A prominently displayed planner at home and in the classroom can help by indicating regular tasks and deadlines.

- ◆ The use of kitchen timers and stopwatches can be used to counteract poor time awareness.

- ◆ Tasks can be planned and the amount of time they need could be predicted.

- ◆ Tasks can be simplified and broken down into small, achievable stages.

All it needs is a little thought and understanding. Lots of others in the class will benefit from this too.

Home–school links

A positive relationship will benefit the child enormously. It is the way that the greatest progress will be made. Everyone working together can give the child joined-up support and focus. It will definitely help parents deal with a condition that they might not understand and which appears to have been visited upon the family out of the blue. It will also bring information back to school that can help in assessment and in targeting support.

Something that is especially important in a condition like dyspraxia, which is not widely recognized, is that parents are reassured that their child's problems are not of their making. It hasn't emerged because of their poor parenting skills. And, as we have seen, you can show them that there are practical solutions that will help.

12

Dyspraxia in the Secondary School

This is an awkward time for all children, for it is a time of change, and change can be unsettling. The difficulties, however, are magnified for a child with dyspraxia. The secondary school is a transitional phase, a move into early adulthood. The agenda might change but the problem of dyspraxia reduces itself to one simple fact: the dyspraxic child can appear to be left behind, stranded in earlier years.

They may not have mastered fastening laces, for example. A simple and relatively unimportant skill in these days of elastic-sided shoes, but one that can assume huge symbolic significance as a task that most of us carry out without thinking and yet one that dyspraxic children can never really get hold of. It can become a representation of their failure. And if others in their class find out about this and start to unfasten the child's shoelaces, what are they to do? If their primary school experience has been unsatisfactory they may already have low self-esteem, which an issue like laces might exacerbate.

The whole purpose of this book is to set a positive agenda and to show how the condition can be managed and how a child with it can achieve. But it has to be acknowledged that the child might have struggled through primary school. The condition might not have been managed and they may not have been treated with sympathy. It is quite possible that they feel rejected by the education process if it has never addressed their needs. The frustration that is felt may well be displayed in poor and disruptive behaviour. It is a very complicated time.

The difficulties of transition

The whole experience of moving to secondary school seems designed to be deliberately confusing. Instead of a small, contained area, the learning environment can be a sprawling mass. Going to school involves moving around almost randomly, in response to an arbitrary timetable of lessons. Their first experience of secondary school could be of a seething mass of older pupils, all knowing where they were going, so unlike the simpler world of the primary school. The registration group will be full of children they do not know, personal space will not be constant. There will more than one table or desk where learning can take place. We want our schools to be interesting and challenging places. The richer the environment the better the school, yet that also means the more opportunities for disaster for a dyspraxic child.

And then there are all those teachers. It would not be unusual if they were meeting male teachers for the first time. Some of these teachers may not have any understanding of, or sympathy for, the condition. They may deal rather harshly with a child they regard as lazy or obstructive. Then there might suddenly be a supply teacher covering for someone familiar, or there will be a teacher who doesn't teach the class very often – say once a week – and so the gap between lessons can make the work all too confusing and all too forgettable. Different faces, different rooms, different tolerances, different expectations.

Many children find this difficult but settle into their new environment in a week or two, but the child with dyspraxia will take much longer. They may feel disorientated and get lost, arriving late to lessons. It will take them much longer to internalize a map and to visualize a pattern of their movements round the school. If they are separated from the others in their class who they have been following all day, then they could become completely disorientated. Unfamiliar teachers who don't know about their condition will shout at them for being in the wrong place when they don't even know where the right place is. The place will seem unfriendly and intimidating, a place designed to be deliberately confusing, a noisy shapeless threat, full of new and unsympathetic demons. They may be taught in bigger groups and that may mean more noise. This increases the chances of being distracted in class. And, of course, as the youngest in the school they have no status at all. They are just fresh meat.

Preparations

It is vital that careful preparations are made by both parents and the school prior to the arrival of children with dyspraxia. All children will benefit from effective liaison, but none more so than those who might be experiencing difficulties.

It is still possible, though increasingly unlikely, that dyspraxia will not have been diagnosed by the time the child starts in secondary school. Generally the secondary school will receive information from the primary school. This information must be distributed so that all staff are aware. Unguarded comments resulting from lack of information can be embarrassing and hurtful.

Proper liaison provides a bridge between primary and secondary school and is designed to ensure there is a continuum linking the two phases. It should ensure that earlier good experiences are built upon and bad ones are not inadvertently repeated. Information needs to be passed on and the child needs to know that this has happened. It is reassurance that in a way their old teachers are still watching over them. Dyspraxic children are no different in this than any other. They all have their stories to tell, and the secondary school experience will be a better one if we listen properly across the key stages.

If the child is to manage the change to secondary school with some success, then the process needs to begin before they even arrive. What the dyspraxic child needs is familiarity, a gradual introduction to this new phase in their life. It might be difficult for a primary school to do this but early visits to the school are crucial, both as part of the class and as an individual. Familiarity is important, so perhaps a support worker can accompany them around the school. Dyspraxics, more than most, will need to be prepared for the movement and the sea of faces. Introductions could be made, both to teachers and to other workers in the school. Of course, the teachers are quite likely to forget over the summer holidays but it is important for the child that these connections have been made. It makes it all seem just a little more familiar. This is an opportunity to find all the important places – the office, the dining hall, the toilets – without the distractions of others.

This process could represent a sense of handing over. Perhaps the support assistant from the primary school could introduce the dyspraxic child to the support assistant in the secondary school. The idea of a familiar and sympathetic face who can act as a point of contact is a very useful one. What is clear is that, in all of this, correctly and imaginatively deployed support workers, well-trained and properly informed, can make a huge difference. They could provide something fixed and familiar in the ever-changing day of our secondary school.

A lot depends upon the sort of induction programme that has been established and how learning advice departments and SENCOs operate. It might be that significant staff will have already visited their partner schools to find things out and to meet significant pupils. This sort of practice blurs the boundaries between the two phases and so makes transition more manageable.

The child needs a plan of the site and the parents need to display it prominently at home. It won't stop problems happening, because we all know that maps are different from reality, but it will develop some familiarity. Parents can be involved by encouraging their children to rehearse the preparations for school and the route to be followed. The summer holiday is a good time to practise going to school!

The emotional minefield

Adolescence can be a difficult time for anyone. The dyspraxic child may encounter additional problems. They will still experience difficulties with physical tasks, sequencing, organization and perception. Handwriting might still be laborious and untidy, though the use of a computer will minimize problems in this area.

One of the important issues that emerges in the adolescent years is body image. Because physical exercise can prove so problematic, a dyspraxic child might avoid it completely. The danger is then that they could become quite unfit, so it is important that they find an activity with which they are comfortable. Swimming is a possibility that is worth exploring since the water will support the body while the relevant movements are arranged and organized. It is a healthy activity that can help the development of effective coordination.

All dyspraxic adolescents will be delighted to learn that computer gaming can make a genuine contribution to an improvement in hand–eye coordination. 'I am not wasting time. I am in therapy'. A very useful or irritating excuse for extended sessions in front of a computer screen, depending on your perspective. But you mustn't dismiss the benefits. Used sensibly, a computer game can offer a safe and enclosed world in which new behaviours and actions can be modelled and the consequences examined. Mistakes can be wiped away and no one, least of all the child, is harmed.

Emotional difficulties will now assume much greater prominence. The child will recently have been one of the oldest in the primary school. This brings with it a certain status. They are expected to set an example and to help the teachers they now know very well and who obviously know them. They will also have been able to mix with the younger pupils in the school, playing with them in an unthreatening environment.

This is the same for all students, whether they are dyspraxic or not. But the effects of growing up place much greater distance between dyspraxics and their peers. Friends who once accepted them for what they are may now perceive something odd and under-developed and move away from them.

The move to secondary school represents an immediate transition from oldest to youngest with a consequent and immediate loss of status. Almost overnight there is no one to play with. Suddenly all their social weaknesses can be exposed. Their failure to keep up with their peers will mark them out as odd. There are not just the usual adolescent issues, the dyspraxic child may have retreated into their own fantasy world, fuelled by the very computer games that could be helping their coordination. The computer and the games console draw them into a controlled and limited world where they can live out lives freed from their frustrations and where, if you make a mistake, you can just start again. They can take risks and model different responses to situations safely. When the real world outside is so complex they may try to avoid it, both emotionally and physically. They might develop a skill at these games but they will have withdrawn into themselves to do so. Everything comes at a price; while they are developing this facil-ity their peers will have moved on. An inability to ride a bike, for example, could mean that they would stay close to home. Not for the dyspraxic is the easy freedom of the streets.

They may not be sociable with any success and so will be neither popular nor cool. Their comments in con-versation may appear tactless or ill-judged. They will struggle to pick up non-verbal signals or misread the tone of others. They might take things too literally.

They will be outside the mainstream. An uncertainty in relationships with their peers can mean that they are not sure how genuine others are, so isolation and loneliness can be inevitable. What becomes important then is the family and the security of home. This in turn emphasizes the differences between themselves and their peers, who all like to pretend that they want to break away.

This inability to read others can make a male adolescence very confusing, since male relationships are often built around teasing and criticism, and if you can't judge your interventions in fast-moving conversation it is going to leave you stranded. The lack of success for a chosen football team can have a devastating effect. As far as you are concerned, the comments of your peers about a defeat is not about the team but about you. It is a very complicated thing to disentangle. In two important areas, sport and teenage conversation, they are likely to be significant underachievers. In these circumstances a boy hasn't much hope.

Is it all bad news?

Well no. There are advantages of course in arriving in a secondary school. It would not have been unusual for a dyspraxic to be the only identified child in their class at primary school. On arrival in secondary school, with a larger population drawn from a range of schools, the child will find that they are not alone. A support group can be established, bringing children together. This can be particularly useful for parents who can then be reassured that they are not alone; they can exchange strategies and advice. The school can take the initiative through the SENCO and bring parents together.

This will also serve to raise the profile of dyspraxia among the rest of the teaching staff of the school. They may then see common features in the children within the group, lending the condition credibility in those areas where it is needed. Subject teachers will be able to see that the condition is genuine. Children too will feel less isolated, less alone and will know more faces around the school as a result.

School transport

This is an important subject that schools will need to consider for those dyspraxic children coming to school particularly in Year 7. Obviously they will need to know where to catch the bus and how to manage either their bus pass or their fare. But the company needs to be advised that the child should sit close to adult supervision. Furthermore, it is unlikely that they'll be able to stand for any length of time. If the transport company is aware of this then it will help to ease understandable parental worries. An older brother or sister or a neighbour could also keep a discreet eye on things. Teachers would be well placed to find a reliable guide who travels on the same route. This kind of 'buddy' support is extremely effective in many different areas, not just on the buses. It is obviously in such unsupervised environments that problems can arise and the school should make every effort to anticipate them.

Sharing the knowledge

The SENCO and the learning advice department should act as a repository of knowledge on dyspraxia and other conditions. They should be able to offer advice and workable strategies across the range of subjects that a secondary school teaches. It is part of their role to keep heads of department or sections aware of all disabilities. It is part of the role of the leadership team to ask departments or sections what they are doing to accommodate the range of disabilities that they face. Staff need to be aware that a child with dyspraxia could well be of above average intelligence but with poor achievement. Once staff are aware of this then they need to do something about it.

It is very difficult for teachers to manage individual learning requirements. They have so much else that demands their attention, examination performance targets for example, so they might well need reminding that an awareness of individual needs is part of their responsibility. Those who are best informed, like the SENCO and the form tutor, will be able to offer appropriate guidance and should be proactive in doing so.

These two people can also provide something that is equally important to the child – a base and a haven for all dyspraxics in the school. If a school can actually establish a physical location for such a base – and it may support children with other difficulties too – then it will help to ameliorate the initial difficulties of transition.

I think the idea of such a support system is worth exploring because it gives a sense of importance to the pupils. It sends out the message: you might find school difficult and the other pupils may not be very sympathetic, but we value you, who you are and what you can do. It is a base, a stable haven in a constantly changing world. It could just be a place to eat sandwiches, but they will always know that it is there – a bolthole, a home.

Classroom assistants, working from this area can then help to disseminate knowledge to subject staff and provide continuity. It can also be a place where they can go when the going gets tough.

Obviously the use of support workers in the classroom is something that needs to be addressed as a whole-school issue. But in the case of dyspraxia, teachers need to be aware that additional adults in a classroom can make an immediate impact. They can mediate between the child and the task, repeating instructions, guiding and structuring. Remember, dyspraxic children will always respond to individual attention.

The importance of the form teacher

The early years of the secondary school could well be the most difficult for the dyspraxic child. Their problems will start to have a greater impact, especially socially. They will have to contend with cruelty and unkindness. Their relationships with their classmates could be difficult. Everything about the school could be disorientating. As a result they will rely a great deal upon relationships with their teachers. The two most important people in the school at this time are likely to be the SENCO and the form teacher. The SENCO will probably help most to manage the condition, the form teacher will help to manage the child. Perhaps this is too simplistic, but it does indicate the real importance of the role of the form tutor.

Dyspraxia

A form teacher or mentor will need to keep in close contact with parents throughout the secondary school career in order to maximize support. They can give advice to parents who might be anxious for their child about what can be done at home. A form teacher will find useful advice in the primary section of this book that they can share. The advice there still pertains, even if the child is a little older, because there is no easy or quick resolution to some of these problems.

Offering advice is what much of teaching is about, usually in the form of advice about academic issues. Teachers know what books to read, what questions to ask. When you start advising on dyspraxia you start to talk about domestic things too and lifestyle issues. Don't be embarrassed about this. It is practical advice that parents will need. They will need to think about things like appropriate and manageable shoes for a child who can't fasten laces and about tricky issues like ties. There will come a point at which it is no longer worth pushing either of these skills. All you will be doing is reinforcing the point that they can't do these things and indeed have little chance of ever mastering them. Better to use Velcro than to make them confront the impossible on a daily basis. Parents will need to know that they have your support in focusing on things that will be more profitable.

There are plenty of things that a form teacher can do that are helpful. For example, the form teacher can make sure that there are plenty of copies of the class timetables available, both in school and at home (on the back of the bedroom door, on the fridge, in the school bag). This can be re-enforced in school every day. The child can be reminded of what lessons they have and where they should go. They can be reminded of the names of the teachers they will see and they can be asked to repeat them.

Does the child have a watch? Do they use it? This is an important part of negotiating the exams that will come to dominate their school experience. They will need practice in wearing one. Many children with dyspraxia have a poor concept of time and they need to make an early start in developing a relationship with it. They need to understand time values – how one period of time is longer than another. Your advice should be to suggest the use of a digital watch, which is easier to read. These also have alarms that can be set to give instant reminders and help to achieve short-term objectives.

You can help in the classroom by providing an egg timer. This is a simple visual device which enables a child to see how much time they have got left. This will also help to develop a sense of time values. Other children in the class might want one too and this will diminish the isolation of the dyspraxic child.

Often what they need is nothing more complicated than time. It is the most precious of our resources but you should always try to find some. Discuss events, encourage them to read newspapers and to watch the news. This will give a structure for conversation and improve their self-esteem. It will allow them to develop a sense of themselves as informed people who others want to talk to.

Don't forget that teachers who don't know much about dyspraxia can make things worse. They can label the child as slow or untidy, they can criticize, they can insist on work being repeated. They might even impose a detention or some other sanction, which will merely be a punishment for having a condition. So dyspraxic children might need someone who understands and who can intervene on their behalf. Staff will notice that the child may do badly in lessons but significantly better in one-to-one situations. A child will relate well to the attention they receive. It allows them to focus without the distractions of peers with whom they have difficulty forming relationships. If teachers know what the reasons are, they can respond and make allowances. It is in these ways that dyspraxic children will achieve status within the student body. They will never achieve that status through physical activity.

As a form teacher, you need to focus on successes and give out positive messages about improvement and success; you need to promote a feel-good attitude. As a support to the child, your comments are crucial. They need to feel that they have an ally and a support in the ever-changing and complicated world of school.

So focus on the positive. Ask them, 'What have you learned today? Tell me one good thing that happened to you yesterday.' The dyspraxic child might not always want to respond; they might not wish to be positive. But you must do it, 'Let's look at what is in the newspaper today.' You must try to shift the focus to good things.

You can hold regular meetings where the child can be given an opportunity to catch up on their work. This would be a particularly productive use of lunchtime, for a dyspraxic child will often spend this period avoiding things. So this sort of space in the day can be really useful, whether provided by the SENCO or the form teacher. And if LSA support can be provided then so much the better. A flexible interpretation of working hours could provide important support. Dyspraxic children will need a moment or two to understand what happened in the morning and get ready for the afternoon. Other things can come out of such a group – an understanding of a pupil's interests and a means of exploiting these interest for example. They will have a secure place in which they could feel confident enough to share their problems and fears.

Of course, as they get older this time can be used very profitably to complete coursework assignments as they might need a little more time to present things successfully. It is good idea to ensure access to a computer for use at this time.

One thing to remember is that time is made available in the primary school for the development of basic skills like handwriting. In secondary school there is often no time set aside for these things; the assumption is made that they have been acquired. What the school requires is speed and legibility. A form teacher can find the time needed perhaps in registration or at break time to practise handwriting. However important word processors have become, they have yet to replace handwriting completely. It doesn't have to be repetitive exercises in letter formation. It could be the copying out of an important piece of text or an interesting news item. Encourage them to take an interest in the wider world; they will eventually find an enthusiasm and an interest with your help – it might be flags or coins or cars. Good support from a form teacher will help them explore it. Such a relationship with a sympathetic adult could be an effective substitute for less satisfactory relationships with the others in their class.

You need to remember this idea of dyspraxia being

a hidden handicap. Even though you can't see it, it doesn't go away. When you have experience of it at first hand, you would never be able to doubt that it exists or that its effects are wide-ranging. That is why you should never give up. The support offered must be sustained, just as it would be for a child with a more visible disadvantage.

Subjects in secondary school

Each subject that is taught in a secondary school has its own arena and its own rules. This means that they have their own particular and perhaps unexpected difficulties. In **science** for example the seating available in a laboratory could make life very difficult for a child with poor balance. They could be concentrating so much on maintaining their balance on a lab stool that they have no idea what is going on in the lesson. Perhaps it would be better for them to stand during any experiments. Indeed in some experiments, particularly in the early years, they could be a positive danger. So it might be better to let them watch rather than expose them to danger and ridicule. Someone – the SENCO or the form teacher – needs to take the initiative to tell the science department in order to preempt any problems. This emphasizes the key point about supporting children with any sort of difficulty – the need for effective and professional communication between schools to begin with and then between departments.

Don't forget that dyspraxic children need to be part of a team, they need the acceptance that this represents. They might begin by having a role to record results, but once they are involved then their role can develop. They can bring lots of positive elements to group work because they interpret the world in a different way. It gives them unexpected insights and eventually this can be a way in which they can establish credibility with other students.

Drama is a subject that could help enormously. The bright lights of the stage might be too uncomfortable, but the opportunity to work behind the scenes in productions or to be involved in improvisation in lessons will help to raise self-esteem. Dyspraxics want to be involved and like the idea of the sort of teamwork that is often denied them because of their condition. They could be extremely useful production assistants and this will give them pleasure and status. They will learn the importance of schedules and timing and clear preparation and organization.

Physical education lessons merit a section all to themselves (see Chapter 13). Children need good, well-structured opportunities to develop confidence and maintain a level of fitness. What the form teacher needs to watch for is that they are neither mocked nor bullied because they can't run very well. Of course, they are quite capable of making things worse for themselves. They might want to be involved in things everyone else says they can't do. In their head they can play football, or netball, or cricket well enough. On the pitch their colleagues don't agree, but they might keep putting their name forward for the class team and keep being rejected. This is not something in which a teacher should interfere and you certainly shouldn't insist that the child is part of a competitive team, for any defeat, rightly or wrongly, will be blamed on them. This will clearly make things worse and they could soon be ostracized. What you should do is find alternatives, where they can help and where they can succeed – in environmental clubs, for example, or on the school magazine or website.

English has significant emotional content, particularly in the study of literature, and can provide an opportunity for the expression of personal feeling and for empathy with characters and situations. It is important to encourage an examination of the feelings of others in the controlled environment that a book provides. An opportunity to focus on ideas and opinions and to contribute in oral exercises is something that they will appreciate. It will help to counteract any difficulties in their standing that confused and untidy handwriting might give them. If their handwriting is a problem then look for the different ways of presenting and recording achievement through technological developments.

Design technology on the other hand is fraught with difficulty, where inadequate control and manipulation could place a child on the cusp of disaster. The idea of a dyspraxic child with a sharp knife in one hand and a slippery onion in the other can send shivers running down your spine and the workshop technician running for the first-aid box.

Once again, the opportunity for teamwork could be very important. The child may not have the appropriate manual dexterity but there are contributions that they can make when they are part of a problem-solving team. They will have insights and solutions because they are indeed different. Contributing towards the successful achievement of an objective will help to build bridges between themselves and others. They can be part of a team that succeeds in a way that is impossible in a sporting context.

In **maths** they may find it hard to line up columns of figures in order to do calculations, so make sure that they have access to squared paper that will stop figures becoming transposed. Remember that any activity involving scissors could prove exceedingly difficult to perform with any accuracy or precision. Such inabilities are quickly picked up by those in the classroom who are less than sympathetic. Tracing or mirror work might present unexpected difficulties and have within them the potential for humiliation. Alternative approaches can always be employed.

Get organized

A carefully arranged strategy for the school day will help enormously, and a teacher can help to establish a successful one. The daily business of school needs to be resolved, as without a careful and thoughtful approach the whole day can become a mess. But, in my view, it is in simple things like personal support and organization that effective solutions to dyspraxia can be found. You don't, however, have to take complete control of their life. Of course the child needs to begin to take some responsibility for these things because this is how they will need to approach the rest of their lives, but a little bit of help at an early age can go a long way.

♦ A transparent pencil case is very useful since it provides a quick and easy check that everything is in place. They are also insisted upon by examination boards as the only cases permitted in the exam room. So start early.

Dyspraxia

♦ Encourage the child to have a place for everything and to put things back properly so that they can be found easily.

♦ Encourage the making of lists of things to do that are then regularly reviewed.

♦ Use a sloping surface for writing to assist clarity and neatness.

♦ Post-it notes are very useful. They can provide instant temporary reminders and can be displayed prominently and in a variety of places.

♦ Remind colleagues to ask dyspraxic children to repeat any instructions they have been given. They should never assume that the child has engaged with the task straightaway.

♦ Encourage children to join groups and school societies.

♦ Use a laptop where possible.

♦ The use of a dictaphone can help in remembering important points and instructions. It could also be a way of beginning to structure written responses.

♦ Encourage the child to talk themselves through a task so that they can engage with the different stages and processes that make it up.

This sort of underpinning will allow them to function both in school and beyond. To see a role model like a teacher giving this sort of advice is very influential.

Making choices

With increasing maturity students will become more involved in their own learning and eventually be in a position where they can make choices about what they are going to study. When they do reach this stage they may well experience a sense of considerable relief. They will be able to put behind them those subjects that have caused them difficulty or embarrassment, such as physical education or art.

These choices do have to be made carefully. They could be intellectually drawn to reflective subjects, which might actually be harder for them, such as history. Here the pressure to produce substantial pieces of written work in a pressured examination performance could bring its own problems. Their disadvantages might preclude them from successful involvement in practical subjects but it doesn't necessarily mean that they will be good at others instead.

An important factor could be that the student may be more comfortable working on their own, at their own pace, so they could perform well in project work. Looking for a subject that gives such opportunities could be profitable.

Every child is individual and so it's impossible to make any broad or definitive judgements and recommend particular subjects. It does seem to me, however, that information technology could be a good choice, since the computer does even things out so that the playing field is, as they say, a little more level, and it will always play an important part in a dyspraxic's school career. Certainly, there is no need, in most circumstances, to make any exemptions from the normal school curriculum for dyspraxics. Work with it, or work around it, don't give in to it.

Work experience

This can be a moment of great significance in the secondary school career. Suddenly the emphasis is upon looking forward towards a future of employment rather than upon daily concerns. It is a time to try out possibilities and to have new, more adult, experiences. It is though a change, and changes bring with them the anxiety of the unfamiliar. Responsibilities for the dyspraxic student might, for the first time, involve managing transport and money for daily expenses. It is a first tentative step into an adult world.

Obviously the hosts need to be fully briefed by the school so that they will know what to expect. It would be wise to ensure that they are aware of any limitations on the student's performance to avoid embarrassment and misunderstanding. The student would suffer considerable distress if they were asked to do something that they couldn't perform because of their dyspraxia. So the placement needs to be chosen with care, because it still needs to be challenging and interesting. Standing by the side of the photocopier, straightening paperclips, does the whole concept of work experience a particular disservice. When this happens it becomes a waste of time, whether you are dyspraxic or not.

An initial visit by the student with a teacher would be helpful. It would also be advisable to give them an opportunity to rehearse any journey that may be unfamiliar before the start of the placement. The location of toilets should be established. Lunch arrangements need to be clarified. A teacher shouldn't forget that it is the basic domestic issues that must be sorted out before a learning experience can happen. Learning can certainly take place and it should be a positive experience. The dyspraxic student has a great deal to gain and the attentions and advice of adults will help them to formulate ideas about their own future. But this can only happen if work experience is properly and thoughtfully planned.

13

Dyspraxia and the PE Teacher

The main reason why physical education should have a section all to itself in this book is because it is such a nightmare area for the dyspraxic child. It could prove to be one of the most stressful periods of their day. Unless they are treated sympathetically and professionally, their sense of self-worth and their world view could be damaged for ever. Also, the improvements that can be achieved through physiotherapy need to be reinforced by the PE teacher back in school.

PE teachers sometimes see themselves as poor relations, overlooked and marginal figures. Here they have an opportunity to play a central role. Dyspraxia is a condition that has a particular physical manifestation. Sympathetic PE teaching is vital to the overall success of the dyspraxic child. It can have an enormous impact on them.

Every PE teacher will have seen an undiagnosed dyspraxic child at some point. The boy who stands there and waits for the cricket ball to hit them before they raise the bat. The girl who is not sure which direction to run in rounders. The child who appears to run as though wearing diving boots. The teacher needs to remember that it is not their fault.

Dyspraxia

Other children around them will be achievers; they will have an instinctive grasp of the skills they need to play games – the hand–eye coordination, the spatial awareness. The great players in any sport always seem to have more time to play than the others around them. Their anticipation and awareness seem so much more enhanced.

The dyspraxic child will stand out – certainly ungainly, possibly inept. Their inability will have inevitable consequences. In team games they will be the last to be picked. In the changing room they may well be the first to be picked on. Given the physical nature of the lesson it can become the ideal area for intimidation and bullying. A pecking order is soon established and an inability in physical things quickly pushes you to the bottom of it.

Boys make judgements about each other often on the basis of their ability in games. It is not an issue a dyspraxic girl must face. Their status can come from their ability to emulate sporting heroes. The dyspraxic boy hasn't a hope. The only achievement that can be guaranteed is that at some point they will let down their team through their ineptitude, and for this a price must be paid.

What they do not need is ignoring, for this will only confirm prejudices and lead inevitably to the bullying to which a dyspraxic child is prone. A particular concern would be the changing rooms where careful supervision is essential to prevent intimidation and humiliation. I know which side of the changing room door the teacher needs to be.

The issues are there for all to see in primary school and they just won't go away. There is the pressure to get dressed and undressed properly and quickly. There will be huge pressure to keep up with the rest of the class. At home there isn't much of a problem because mum or dad can help, but such problems can persist into secondary school. If laces become involved then everything can fall apart very quickly, and in a public arena. They will be instantly exposed. The PE teacher must minimize such difficulties.

The activities involved in the lesson can be very difficult and stressful. The child's ball skills may be non-existent, climbing onto benches and apparatus can be daunting. The PE lesson can hang over them like a black cloud – a constant and public reminder of their inabilities. They won't be indifferent to PE. They will hate it. They will avoid it at any cost, truanting from school if that is the only way to escape the humiliation. Dealing with the impatience of others in team situations will haunt them throughout the week. Their differences will be accentuated and their feelings of inadequacy reinforced by the hurtful comments of their peers.

It is important that they are not humiliated in physical activity. They need encouragement and PE staff, who are clearly achievers themselves, can do a great deal to ensure the preservation of self-esteem. Their successes need praising and they need the attention and respect of the teacher. As role models for others, teachers always have a particular responsibility. Let's have a look at possible strategies that could be employed.

♦ A dyspraxic child will find kicking a ball very difficult. They will be unable to direct it accurately and will struggle to make judgements about how hard the ball needs to be kicked. Skills can be improved by using a large foam ball to show direction and the amount of force required.

♦ The child may be unable to stand on one leg and may be extremely inefficient when running. Trampolining can help balance and swimming can aid coordination and sequencing. These exercises should eventually have some impact on running.

♦ Swimming provides an opportunity to form physical movements while supported by the water. It is an activity they can take part in at their own pace. And it is a physical activity they can carry with them into the rest of their life.

♦ PE can do a great deal to improve handwriting through the use of directional games, reinforcing the concept of left to right movement. It will also help with the concept of order and direction. Movement to music will help by giving a structure to movement and so help with the rhythm required for efficient handwriting.

♦ The teacher should try to develop a positive attitude in the dyspraxic child towards PE by offering encouragement and attention. Given the difficulties they face, there is a real danger that the dyspraxic child could become extremely unfit, with inevitable consequences for their long-term health. They might spend the rest of their life avoiding physical activity as a result of scars unwittingly acquired at school. Exercise is vital for their future well-being.

♦ The child will know that they are not as good as others, so they don't need white lies about how good they are – they will know they are being patronized. They need realism. So the focus should be upon how they have improved upon past performance.

♦ The best sorts of instructions are simple ones. Don't issue too many in one go. Break down any physical actions into simple steps. Remember too that they may have difficulty in absorbing the rules for any new game. Keep those as simple as you can.

♦ Make sure that the child can hear and see instructions clearly. Also make sure that they are at the front and not peering at you from the back. They will find it extremely hard to maintain concentration if they are. You might find it helpful to ask the child to repeat the instructions to the class as a whole, to remind both the class and themselves. This will also grant small but important status.

♦ Obviously don't ask dyspraxics to provide a physical example of an activity. This could further undermine their already fragile self-esteem.

♦ Consider the use of different activities for dyspraxic children as warm-up exercises. The more fun and interesting they are, the more other children will want to join in. This is a good way of breaking down barriers. In a secondary school it might even be something as simple as using beanbags. They are often better than balls.

♦ Most activities can suit any age group if simple alterations are made. Younger children could indeed use a beanbag for throwing and catching. An older child would probably seek to avoid humiliation by wanting to work with a ball. Of course, there are many sorts of balls, from foam ones which are light and don't travel too fast but don't bounce either, to hedgehog balls which are hard but help children to grip. Volleyballs are much better than the heavier basketballs as they don't hurt if catches are missed. And of course, involving the whole class in an activity using a specific ball shelters the dyspraxic child, and others similarly less confident, from ridicule.

♦ Skittle Alley is an activity that can be beneficial. Rolling a ball to knock down skittles helps aiming and coordination. All children can be involved by taking turns at the different activities involved. Some children can bowl the ball and others can be in charge of replacing the skittles, while others still keep the score. Alleys can be constructed with benches to contain the ball so that poor aiming isn't immediately made apparent by the ball going to the side. Skittles can be made from plastic bottles half-filled with sand or water if the game is outside. They can then judge and measure how much water has been lost when the skittle falls over. Younger children can make lighter skittles which will topple more easily.

♦ Basketball can be fun and popular with all classes. Waste-paper baskets tied to wall bars are excellent for learning to aim and developing a sense of distance and direction. The action involves an overhand push and so it is important to establish the correct stance by having the opposing foot forward to create a stable platform for the action. The distance between the child and the basket can, naturally, be varied and a competitive element can be included if you wish.

♦ An important point is to offer a more imaginative range of activities – Pilates, yoga, t'ai chi could all help posture.

♦ Be aware that some children with dyspraxia might have poor posture and be unable to sit unsupported. Sitting cross-legged on the floor could be impossible for them.

♦ Try to minimize situations in which the child is chosen last when selecting teams. Many of us without dyspraxia remember the shame of being the one whom no one wanted in their team. Now imagine what it must be like to be regularly humiliated in this way. Dyspraxic children mustn't be excluded. Appropriate involvement in team games will impact upon status and social skills.

What must not be forgotten is that properly structured and thoughtful physical activities can make a huge impact on the development of gross motor function. However, motivation might be a problem. Why should they humiliate themselves in front of others? What purpose does it serve? The child might need to be encouraged to take part and to put their apprehensions to one side. To do this they will need to feel secure and valued. Activities like crawling and skipping can lead to measurable improvement. Swimming has been found to be especially beneficial. There are simple things that can mean so much and can lead to a real improvement in the condition and in the way the child is seen by himself and by others. This is the challenge that the dyspraxic child presents to all PE teachers, whatever age range they teach. If they are switched on to their professional responsibilities a PE teacher will know what to do. They have a status among the great unwashed of the student body. And that pack of wolves might take their lead from the toned achiever in the tracksuit.

The PE teacher must embrace the dyspraxic. It is their role. It is their duty. They must never give off any signal, however unconsciously, that the dyspraxic child is not worthy of attention. They must be nurtured, they must get attention, they should be given tasks to perform. They could become the trusted companion with important responsibilities, the kit-man, the scorer to the team.

It is really important to give them this status and the approval of a high-profile teacher. Get them involved, show that they are important, and you will be helping them to build relationships with those who might otherwise have tried to humiliate them. It is not usually the German teacher who is best placed to do this; it is the PE teacher.

14

Examinations

Formal assessment plays a huge part in education. We have oral assessment, coursework and we have examinations. These are the ways in which we register judgements about a child's abilities and we draw conclusions from them. Exams are extremely influential, determining jobs, careers and education. Indeed, our whole system of education is built upon examinations. They are the focal point for most of the teaching that any child receives. So a school, all schools, must have in place strategies that help dyspraxics achieve results that confirm their abilities rather than reveal their dyspraxia.

There are three distinct phases to education as far as examinations are concerned. You need to put the information in: that is the teacher's job. The information has to be stored: that is the job of the student. Then it all has to be churned out at the right time and under pressure. You can see the problem here. Dyspraxic children can struggle with all three different areas. But the student's responsibility to store and then retrieve the information is a significant area of weakness.

The student who wants to succeed and feels positive because of the support they have received in school will be best placed to achieve success in examinations. The dyspraxic child will need help to organize and to plan. This has to be a central message in everything to do with dyspraxics. They have difficulty in doing this, so teachers need to get involved and help them to do it. After all, the secret to examination success at any age lies in careful preparations.

Here are some suggested ways to help prepare:

♦ Create a timetable and a study programme in the run-up to the examinations.

♦ Subject teachers should provide an overview of topics studied as a reminder. Identify key points or ideas that could act as a trigger for more detailed information.

♦ Shorter, intense periods will be more productive than longer, more diffuse sessions of revision for a student who finds concentration difficult.

♦ Encourage the use of highlighters to bring colour to the body of notes that have to be learned. Colours can be used to identify themes or issues.

♦ Use Internet resources to add variety and visual interest to revision.

♦ They need to be given examples of the kind of tasks they will need to fulfil. This sort of modelling will help to provide a structure that they might not be able to find within themselves.

♦ Don't forget that they are often highly intelligent people with a specific but significant difficulty. You need to help them overcome it and so succeed.

Coursework is always going to play to the strengths of the dyspraxic student, especially in the age of computers. They should be encouraged to achieve the highest marks possible in this element, which will compensate for any slight underachievement in time-determined situations. Sadly, coursework may be slipping away because there are increasing problems with authenticity. In the digital world written work can fly around the Internet so swiftly, and we live in a world where students can cut and paste their way to success. But for dyspraxic candidates we need to hang on to it for as long as we can.

A teacher can help a great deal by providing a structure for any coursework. Many people find it very difficult if they are presented with a blank sheet of paper. They need a framework, a way of breaking down a longer piece of work into smaller, manageable sections, smaller objectives leading to something more significant. It would be important to start early on in the course. Explain the requirements and get parents involved if you can; they might want to help with field trips for example. There is no reason why they shouldn't go along, if appropriate, to support their child. This would then enable parents to repeat the field trip at a later date if necessary. As we have noticed all along, we are not talking about particular strategies for dyspraxics alone. This is just good teaching.

There needs to be a programme of study skills that will show students how to learn. They might need to relate knowledge to visual clues by designing word maps or spider diagrams. You can make tapes of revision material that can be played on a personal stereo. You can record files onto your computer as MP3 files that can be played on MP3 players – revision on the move. School websites today often include revision material that can be accessed from home and often they are in the form of audio files. These things can be extremely effective. Everything needs to be designed to develop confidence and to make material familiar and internalized.

Fundamentally, what you must do as a teacher is to help the student manage all the information that is thrown at them on a daily basis. You need to help them filter it and process it. You need to help bring order to the chaos.

Once you have developed the techniques required to help the dyspraxic student learn and revise, you need to help them structure their approach in the examination room.

A response to pressure is a very individual thing. Some people thrive in examinations, enjoying the focus and purpose it gives to the work they have done, others feel overwhelmed by the experience. What is obvious is that teachers themselves must in general have been good at examinations. We can speak about them with authority because if we hadn't been good at them then we would never have achieved the qualifications to become teachers in the first place. So we must be sympathetic and try to understand the difficulties that others are facing.

The dyspraxic child is likely to need support if their self-confidence is low as a result of the frustrations of their education. They could approach exams with foreboding.

The exams will be difficult; there are no two ways about that. The nature of examinations does not play to their strengths. The pressure to work quickly, to plan and organize, are precisely the things they have always needed help with. They may find it hard to deal with their own anxiety, they may find it hard to recall information in the correct order, they may struggle to write quickly and legibly. What they will need is a strategy for approaching the examination experience. Teachers should have plenty of advice to offer, since in many ways examinations are what their job is about.

Individual training sessions could be very useful. Tutorials and individual meetings will help dyspraxics to concentrate and to plan their revision. Ensure they have a revision plan and schedule written in diary form. 'Monday 5–6pm History. 7–8pm Maths.' That sort of thing.

Here are some other suggestions:

◆ Break down revision into manageable chunks.

◆ Propose a plan to negotiate the entire exam. Indicate in which order questions should be attempted.

◆ Focus on how to use the available time. Specify how long should be spent on particular questions.

◆ Try to ensure that someone is there at the start of the examination just to offer reassurance and to calm apprehensive students. A familiar face, telling everyone that the exam is fine can be important for everyone.

◆ A check can also be made that the necessary equipment has been brought.

◆ There is no reason why you shouldn't write the time plan out and display it at the front of the examination room for the benefit of everyone. So you could write '10.10am start question 2. 10.35am start question 3.' Tell the dyspraxic student when the exam has reached these points, or adapt the advice for them if they are entitled to extra time in which to complete their answers.

♦ If appropriate, provide dyspraxic candidates with a separate room so that they will not be distracted by others and will have more success in maintaining fragile concentration.

♦ It is vital that examination invigilators are fully informed about the dyspraxic students and their entitlement to extra time. It is their duty to ensure that the students receive it.

This last point is an important one. It is likely that any statement of special educational needs will indicate that the dyspraxic child can have additional time in examinations. For some this will be no help, since all it will do is prolong the agony. This is a significant point here. The statement might say that they need the time, but practising teachers will know if it helps or not. The reality is that, however well-meaning it appears, for some it is a waste of time. However, for others it may allow them to flourish. You need to reassure the student that there is no shame in accepting this allowance. Many children are reluctant to take the time, even if they are entitled to it. They feel embarrassed, singled out, different, when all their school career they have tried to be the same. But if it is their entitlement then they should have it. Teachers will need to speak to dyspraxic students at an early stage about this and perhaps involve parents.

Examinations

It might be wise to consider taking 'mock' or preparatory examinations without any additional time allowance to assess how the student performs when writing under time pressures. This will provide evidence for any discussion that might be needed. Then, if extra time is felt to be useful, give them an opportunity to practise with this concession in internal examinations. It is not really something that should be sprung upon them when they arrive at the real SATS or GCSE examinations.

15

Education beyond 18

Like many young people, the dyspraxic student might view college and university with a sense of liberation. Finally they will be able to put behind them all the frustrations and forget the things that reminded them of their inadequacies and concentrate on what they can do. They can make choices about what to do and how to do it. Some will be all too eager to leave school, where they have always confronted failure, but they need to be encouraged to think carefully. They shouldn't reject education too soon. What sort of future will they have without it? It is important to arrest any sort of decline that can lead to frustration and antisocial behaviour. There are, for example, higher levels of dyslexia in the prison population, with huge ongoing costs to society, and there is every reason to assume that the position is much the same with dyspraxia. It is important that everyone gives off encouraging messages at school. Incidents of bullying should by now be in decline, though there will still be a residual lack of confidence as a result of a hard time in the secondary school. At this stage there is less of a requirement to conform, as teenage lifestyle fractures into a whole host of possibilities. In the early part of secondary school everyone had to be the same. Now everyone wants to be different.

Dyspraxia

But of course it is never so straightforward. Choices bring stressful interludes and the move towards greater independence can be haphazard. But leaving school is another change and it can be managed with help in the same way other transitions are managed. Knowledge and preparation are the keys.

Support will be needed in filling in application forms and in preparing CVs but this is normally offered to all students anyway. They may need a number of attempts at it but easy correction and revision is one of the familiar benefits of the electronic system that now processes applications. Once again there must be an emphasis upon the transfer of information. The form tutor, who has we hope established a working relationship over a number of years, needs to feel confident someone else will be stepping into their role.

Naturally this transition brings with it issues about self-support. All parents fret about this but with dyspraxic students there are added concerns and important decisions to discuss.

♦ Is the student ready to leave home and deal with a new way of life?

♦ Can they deal with a new environment, with the need to form new relationships with students and tutors?

♦ Would the student benefit more from studying in their home town rather than moving away?

♦ Or should the emphasis be upon somewhere that is easily accessible?

These are big decisions and an informed teacher can make a helpful contribution to the debate. A particular issue that could be explored is whether grants and allowances are available for students with dyspraxia. A lot depends upon their statement of educational needs. Teachers should consult their LEA and the DfES for the current position. It may be that Disabled Student's Allowance would be available. This is not means-tested and is a grant not a loan, so it doesn't have to be repaid. The student might be eligible to receive recorders or computer equipment. The financial implications of this can be quite significant. It might also be helpful to contact individual institutions to see what they can do. Some of them have their own schemes and as a teacher you should advise students and parents to pursue them.

Most higher education institutions will have study advisers who will be available to assist students in their learning. It might be good advice to suggest that your dyspraxic student makes contact with one soon after their arrival. It is a way of ensuring that the relevant information has indeed been passed on. It might also be the way to pursue the Disabled Student's Allowance if it hasn't already been granted.

At least your student will have developed compensatory techniques over the years to manage the condition. Other students though may not have been recognized and may have been compensating unconsciously. Their difficulties might suddenly become amplified when they are thrown into a new environment, having to live independently and meet new academic standards. Your student certainly won't be alone and might, in fact, be in a better position than others.

Dypsraxia

Even if financial assistance isn't forthcoming, other levels of support can be accessed, particularly with regard to assessment procedures (exams, course-work, dissertations, etc.) and technical support (laptop computers that need to be configured). So it is definitely worth doing. It is another example of how communicating information can be so important.

All those stages that were required when the transfer was made between primary and secondary school all those years ago need to be replayed, with the intention of developing familiarity with a new environment and the demands that it will make. The issues may be slightly different, that's all.

They will need to find their way around this new space. It will all be unfamiliar and they might start bumping into things. Narrow aisles between shelves in libraries might be difficult places to manage. They might need to spend a lot of their time there. They will also need to maintain their habit of making lists and reminders. There is always the danger that they might miss appointments for seminars or they might forget about the milk in the fridge. The need for careful organization will always be there, only there will now be different things to it:

- Does the student have a timetable for changing and washing clothes?

- Is the student ready to start managing money? Can they remember not to go to the cash machine too often?

- Does the student have a filing system for storing notes so that they can be easily retrieved?

146

♦ Have they been sent away with birthday cards already addressed and labelled that merely need posting so that they don't forget those important family milestones?

All those things for which they previously relied upon others for help will become pressing issues when they become their own responsibility.

Schools will also need to prepare for interviews, especially for the dyspraxic child who is not socially adept. It is inevitable that the inability to recognize facial expressions in a conversation or interview, the inability to maintain good eye contact or the shambling walk and slumped body shape, the weak handshake, will all give an impression that the student is not sociable. Immediately inaccurate conclusions may be drawn. Naturally, their clumsiness, their failure to pick up on clues in a conversation will be less of a problem if the prospective institution has been made aware of the condition and knows to some extent what to expect. In the liberal and learning atmosphere of a college or university you should be confident that they will receive a sympathetic welcome.

It is an exciting time for everyone, and brings with it worry as well as opportunity. With careful and sensitive planning it can be managed successfully.

Higher or further education is a huge thing for the family and with a dyspraxic child the normal anxieties of a parent are magnified. They can see that this change in their child's life could be enormously beneficial and that it should happen, but they can't see how their child will be able to do it. A wide range of issues will consume the parent's fretful hours.

Dyspraxia

The apprehension that parents feel could be allayed to some extent by ensuring that the institution acknowledges difficulties and gives some priority to making sure accessible and suitable accommodation is available. Most will try to ensure that those with more pressing needs are suitably supported. As always, the key here is effective communication between institutions. This has been shown to be important at every stage.

You need to ensure that the appropriate information is passed on. You would certainly wish to avoid any possibility of the dyspraxic student you have nurtured for seven years in secondary school suddenly finding themselves in self-catering accommodation with a kettle and pot noodles.

It is really important that you encourage parents and students to take advantage of the open days organized by most higher and further education institutions. It is an excellent opportunity for them to familiarize themselves with this potential, and new, environment. They can meet equally confused and nervous students who are apprehensive about an unfamiliar future. At the same time they will be able to recognize the excitement of these future opportunities, and it can happen in a controlled and structured situation with parents in attendance. It is a gentle introduction and a good way of glimpsing the future. It is a vision of what the future can be and perhaps a spur to achievement.

Of course, dyspraxic students might not have a clue about what it all will mean. They may have wildly unrealistic expectations of their own capabilities. Teach a dyspraxic a simple dish like a stir-fry with some noodles and suddenly in their eyes they have mastered all aspects of cooking, when you might be more concerned that they can slice things without losing a digit. Looking at accommodation and catering alternatives can provide a focus and an opportunity to engage, however casually, with a future that contains the cold reality of a pile of dirty underwear that needs the attention of a too-distant parent. To the usual teenage refusal to engage with what they see as irrelevant detail, you must add the emotional immaturity of dyspraxia.

Stay practical. If there is a need to chop, it can be negotiated with sensible expenditure on ready-sliced meat and veg from the supermarket.

A parent's apprehension may be multiplied because of their child's unsustainable fantasies that go beyond their expertise as a chef. When your whole life might have been sustained by an imaginary world into which you have regularly retreated, then it can be difficult to get a focus on the essential details of living a semi-independent life. Washing. Going to bed. Getting up. Bedding. Sock management. All these are decisions that in the past dyspraxic children have been told to make. Now who is there to make them?

Their ability to cope with others who might be less than sympathetic or who might wish to exploit them, for whatever reason, will always be a major concern. They will be awash with the same emotions as the rest of us, yet even less able to deal with them. What chance is there of them being able to be equal partners in a relationship? It seems to me that they usually *react* to events, as a consequence of the crucial delays that take place in their thought processes, but they are unable to *control* them or to take the initiative. This means that they will usually respond rather than influence or direct.

Dyspraxia

They will see going to university as a time to make new friends, an opportunity perhaps they have longed for after so much difficulty at school, but they might not have the experience or the understanding of how to do it. They will need to plug themselves into a new network but they will probably have no one there to help them do it. Their response to those who show an interest in them can be too enthusiastic. Their ability to build friendships and to interpret others is thin. Years of being ridiculed or rejected can give them an air of desperation. And if they are going to find it hard to make relationships, how are they ever going to be able to end them?

We have all known people like this. It is part of the emotional soup in which we live. We see their inept grasp of social skills and think little of it. We move on. Perhaps these people are undiagnosed dyspraxics. It is not our problem. When that excruciating clumsiness in social situations that features in the work of many comedians is a reality for someone we love, then it stops being funny.

In the end, the dyspraxic child just seems so vulnerable. Both student and parents will require the support of a familiar and informed teacher at this important time. It might be the end of your relationship with a student whom you have watched change and grow. As a professional you will want this final transition to be comfortable and successful, and you will remember yourself that learning is just a small part of going away from home to study.

Of course it is a big step, and as a teacher you must encourage it. None of us should ever accept the possibility of unfulfilled potential without a genuine and sustained struggle. If the dyspraxic student has the ability, then extending their studies will be the central part of their development as a person. What other opportunity will they ever have of leaving home and growing properly without it? Without it what will they become?

16

Into Adult Life

This book is designed to inform teachers so as to ensure that they are best placed to deal with the dyspraxic children that they meet. Thus strategies for adult sufferers fall outside its remit. However, teachers will want to know what will happen to the children with whom they have built close relationships during school years. After all, teachers are preparing their students for the complexities of adult life, both within academic study and beyond. They will want to be in a position to offer practical help and guidance. It is what teaching is about. That is why teachers want, and need, to be informed. This is the great unspoken fear of parents. What sort of future can they expect?

Well, the condition does not go away. It continues into adult life. But it is certainly possible to adapt to its features. There will be some measurable improvements as sufferers mature. There could indeed be a maturation of parts of the central nervous system. The most important thing that happens however is that the dyspraxic finds ways of dealing with the condition. They will specialize in the things that they can do well and avoid other activities. When you are at school, school things seem to be important; when you are older the inability to kick a ball is largely irrelevant.

Dyspraxia

So they learn to operate successfully within the parameters that the condition has established. They adapt their lives, limit their expectations. Perhaps in the end we all do this. All of us have to deal with very complex lives. We accept this and we establish a routine to manage it. A dyspraxic adult might need longer to establish a schedule but in needing a carefully arranged routine they are no different from the rest of us.

Recent technological initiatives have been centred upon making our lives easier. So we have dishwashers, automatic cars, electric carving knives, computers, all designed to even out the differences between us. A carefully managed home environment will ensure an effective lifestyle for a dyspraxic adult. They might need some initial support in learning how to manage money. DIY and cooking could prove problematic, but there are approaches and adaptations that can be employed which are preferable to complete avoidance. It might take them longer to develop independent living skills but these will eventually emerge with support.

If we think about driving for a moment we can see how it is today regarded as an essential skill for life. Now think about the skills that are involved – judging distances, using hands and feet in a coordinated manner, remembering a sequence of events. These are all things that a dyspraxic finds difficult.

But the pressures to learn to drive can be great. It is such an important part of so many jobs and parents may be anxious that their child could become effectively disenfranchised or indeed unemployable. As a teacher you will need to offer advice. There is help available for learner drivers who have coordination difficulties. Information can be found about assessment centres that offer help to drivers with different disabilities. Details can be obtained from the Department of Transport's Mobility Advice and Vehicle Information Service that has the rather fetching acronym of MAVIS. The simulators offered by some driving schools can be a big help because they provide a safe environment for initial learning. Many places offer off-road driving lessons in places like old airfields, which are, once again, secure places to practise and develop skills. You should also remind the student to ask for extra time to complete the written test. It is no different from any other assessment process.

There are other simple strategies too, for instance learning in an automatic car. Advise students to write down any directions they need and stick them to the dashboard, or suggest that they invest in a satellite navigation system. Mark 'left' and 'right' on the steering wheel. There are solutions to most difficulties if imagination and knowledge are employed. However, if a dyspraxic person feels that they are an obvious danger on the road then their wish to avoid driving altogether needs to be respected. They will know what they can do and what they shouldn't attempt.

A more important focus must be upon establishing supportive relationships and satisfying employment. Jobs requiring some sort of manual dexterity won't be feasible but there are plenty of other opportunities. Lives so far spent in dealing with emotions and relationships mean that dyspraxics are sometimes drawn towards caring professions. They have a natural sympathy for others who may be in difficulties. It is often suggested that they are good at looking after animals.

Dyspraxia

The relationship between carer and animal is clearly defined and, apart from sharp teeth and claws, largely unthreatening.

Some dyspraxics can empathize well with others with problems, which means that they can be skilled in careers like caring or social work or teaching. When you consider their legendary handwriting problems, it should not be a surprise to learn that lots of doctors believe that they have been undiagnosed dyspraxics.

We must not forget that here will be things at which they will be very good. They might have acquired good verbal ability or advanced computer skills as a compensatory mechanism. The fact that they have always needed to be very organized could mean that they can flourish in a structured environment like an organization or a bureaucracy.

Their aspirations need to be linked to their intelligence rather than their past experiences in school. Careers advice that is informed and has an understanding of the condition and the student's needs is paramount, especially if the steps into adult life are to be made with some confidence. To ensure that this advice is available, information shared and communication established between different agencies is vital.

The baleful influence of dyspraxia shouldn't be dismissed lightly. Dyspraxia can lead to periods of depression because a lack of self-esteem may have become well established. Social isolation is a state from which escape can be very difficult. Problems in establishing relationships could lead to further loneliness and withdrawal. Adult dyspraxics can be prone to anxiety, nicotine dependence or alcohol abuse. Sadly specialist treatment may be required.

Don't forget, the condition never goes away. And you can see the unequal struggle yourself. You can see that there isn't an even playing field. You can see that it might all become too much. It definitely is not an easy condition.

It can be difficult for dyspraxic sufferers to fulfil traditional gender roles within a relationship. Whatever qualities they have – and they have plenty, like fidelity and loyalty – they are not those that advertisers like to promote. The path towards achievement as a domestic goddess is strewn with difficulties for most and even more so for anyone with coordination difficulties. Similarly the role of the wise and skilled man with a range of clever screwdrivers will be almost impossible to adopt. Yet these are the images that the media promotes, even in these modern and allegedly enlightened times. They will be unable to conform to the stereotype even if they want to and may thus continue to feel a failure. When it comes to caring for children, difficulties with dyspraxia can be exacerbated through the guilt of not being the perfect and coordinated parent and role model.

There is the additional worry that dyspraxics can be easily manipulated by their partners. The result may be that they will tolerate emotional or physical abuse simply because they don't see a way out of their situation. They could feel unable to live successfully as a single person and remain in an unsatisfactory relationship because they believe that they can't cope on their own. They will feel that they have no choices. There are no hard and fast statistics to support this view but anecdotal evidence from dyspraxic organizations would suggest that sufferers are often victims of domestic violence, both male and female. Is it any wonder that a parent's anxiety never really fades?

There are those who speak of the 'gift' of dyspraxia. As the father of a dyspraxic son I am not sure I can agree with this. If it is a gift then it is that jumper with the orange diagonal stripes that you never wanted. I have had to watch my son wade through a deep river while others stride confidently across the bridge just a little way upstream. It seems so unfair.

If you are born with dyspraxia then that is the path that you must follow. We can ease the journey, but we can't change it. Yes, it is unfair but you can't select an alternative. This is no excuse for fatalism.

A positive outlook is essential if serious difficulties are to be minimized. What are you going to do otherwise? Suggest that the student is invited to wallow forever in the swamp of misery? Of course not.

As a teacher you need to remain positive and focus on success and achievement rather than dwelling upon the things that can't be done. It is hard but you must be positive and upbeat. This is your duty. Neither you nor the student nor the parents should get themselves locked into a downward spiral of despair. Without this positive spin the student will have no clear idea of where their strengths lie.

We all need to take the responsibility to ensure that they leave school with a belief that they have a future to look forward to in which they can succeed. Real difficulties lie ahead in a future which is complex and uncertain, but no one should surrender to such difficulties. Fight and the world fights with you; do nothing and you suffer alone.

17

Diet

One positive and potentially effective thing that a dyspraxic person can do is to examine all the implications of a healthy diet. Don't let any dyspraxic you teach do nothing about what they eat and instead accept the poison that is fast and processed food. They need to make conscious decisions about what they eat and be aware of the implications of the choices they make. Even when they think that the world is against them, there are undoubtedly lots of possibilities for genuine improvement by looking at the area of diet and dietary supplements.

Research does indicate that some supplements can have a beneficial effect. The suggestion is that learning and behaviour can be improved by the addition of highly unsaturated fatty acids to the diet, especially the essential fatty acid Omega-3. Evening primrose oil tablets and cod liver oil are both said to reduce dyspraxic difficulties. A child may not be ready to take these things in their natural form, or indeed ready to take them in sufficient quantity, but it doesn't matter because you can take them in pill form.

It is important, however, to keep things in perspective. There are too many people out there making outlandish claims. There is, as yet, no cure for dyspraxia, but it is possible that the effects can be ameliorated, and one of the simplest ways of achieving these changes is through a carefully chosen diet.

Evidence suggests that increasing the amount of fatty acids in the diet can have a discernible impact. There is some sense to this as a large proportion of the human brain is made up of fats, especially Omega-3 fatty acids. The argument is that to increase consumption boosts the brain and so helps it to repair itself. The inadequate connections will firm up and become paragons of efficiency. Our ancestors, after all, ate a very different diet, dependent upon what they could hunt or gather, things like oily fish, wild meat, leafy vegetables, nuts. These things are rich in Omega-3 fats in a way that a modern diet is not. They were feeding their brains. We are not. Let's start feeding them again.

Indeed trials in Durham provided significant evidence for this. A sample of dyspraxic children was selected and half of them were given Omega-3 fish oils and the other half received olive oil. When they were assessed after three months, it was found that those who had taken the active ingredients had made significant, and in some cases quite dramatic, improvements in areas like reading and spelling as well as in handwriting and concentration. Similar tests were carried out at a young offenders' prison in Aylesbury. Those who were given the fish oils had a 30 per cent lower rate of reoffending than those who had the olive oil.

Capsules are not the only way to guarantee adequate access to these fatty acids. They occur naturally in oily fish like herrings and salmon, in tree nuts and oils. They can help to deal with depression, heart disease, cancer, dementia. Although these oils are a help, they aren't a cure, but by dealing with deficiencies in nutrients you are giving the body a chance to fight back by making sure that it runs on optimum fuel.

We are what we eat, as they say. Feed the brain. It doesn't make sense to allow the brain anything other than the very best. When there are doubts about how it is working then why compromise? We must do what is right.

Brain function is also linked to iron levels. It is possible that low levels of haemoglobin mean that there is a reduced oxygen supply to the brain, resulting in impaired brain function. This is important for any child, but it is doubly important for the dyspraxic child. They must be given a chance by making sure they have a healthy diet.

So if you have a dyspraxic student in your class, suggesting a radical dietary review would be a sound strategy. It is certainly not going to do any harm. After all, the main advantage of a healthy lifestyle is that it is good for you. It will bring many other benefits, so the advice must always be to eat proper food.

There is a growing acceptance that too much of our national diet is adulterated. Chemical additives are used to give colour or to flavour foods with inferior ingredients. What is the long-term effect of these things? Food additives are known to fuel temper tantrums and hyperactivity. You will have heard the arguments. Foods which are high in sugar and heavily processed carbohydrates are quickly absorbed by the body and encourage us to eat more. Processed foods have been washed and bleached of all goodness and contribute to nutritional deficiencies. The point, surely, is this. Even if it has a neutral effect why bother with it? We all need food that will help us and when the right stuff is there then why substitute other food which, at best, has no influence at all? And of course if it has a negative effect then it is obvious that it must be avoided. ADHD symptoms have been allieviated in patients who have excluded from their diets additives such as tartrazine, sunset yellow, and sodium benzoate that are all used as dyes. And if care thus needs to be taken with this condition, then surely such care should be exercised with other conditions which exist in the same spectrum?

There is a general acceptance that these things are true. But the answer often presented suggests a need for more commercial dietary supplements. To be honest there would seem to be a great deal of smoke and mirrors involved in these nutritional issues. How much of it can be proved? How much is wishful thinking? How much is motivated by profit? There is a whiff of the patent medicine about all this. 'Apply my snake oil. Visit my clinic. I can also cure baldness by the way and that bottle over there will work wonders on your arthritis and in the back I have just the thing for impotence.' Nothing changes. I used to watch a man with a routine like this every Saturday in Sheffield market when I was a child.

There are difficult issues here I think. Parents want to believe that there is a special syrup on a spoon that will make everything all right. Sadly such a thing is not likely ever to exist. But as a symbol of concern, as a commitment to change and to improvement, a dietary review can be very important, My son took evening primrose oil religiously for years. I don't know whether it made a difference. All I could do was hope that it wasn't doing him any harm. The important thing was that he always felt that it was making a difference. It was his acknowledgement of his condition and came to represent his investment in his own future. As a result, it never really mattered whether the influence these tablets had was genuine or not. He was doing something as a part of a desire to have a healthy lifestyle. Because it is only through having a healthy lifestyle that a dyspraxic child has a chance of establishing a fulfilling adult life.

My opinion, for what it is worth, is that it is better to develop a whole strategy for dealing with the condition that brings together exercises and healthy living, rather than seeking out a magic fountain in an unknown land from which you will drink deeply to make everything better.

As I write this, it is accepted that essential fatty acids are important to the development of the nervous system. They have an important role to play. Additional research is now said to indicate that taking a little zinc sulphate enhances the performance of the essential fatty acids in the building of neuro-transmitters that are responsible for switching information round the brain. In fact, it might regulate the function of the neuro-transmitter dopamine. Dopamine signalling might be something that we should explore. So zinc supplements are big news today. There will be different big news tomorrow.

And I have to be honest. To a layman like myself much of this seems to be complete guesswork. But it doesn't generally seem to do any harm and as a symbolic commitment it is fine. We know there is a problem and we are prepared to take it seriously.

Dyspraxia

In the end, however, you must accept that you are a teacher, not a pharmacist. You need to know about these things in the broadest terms, but you are not the one making the decisions. All you should do is to raise the importance of diet. These are the things you should stress: eat properly, eat sensibly, avoid junk. Help the machine to work properly. If there is anything else you want to do then carry out some careful research beforehand and take professional advice.

Personally, I have yet to be convinced that there is anything more effective than sensible and informed management as a means of alleviating the effects of dyspraxia.

18

Feeding the Brain

If we look after the brain then we are giving ourselves a chance of dealing with any condition that is disrupting the way that it works. We must look after our brains just as we look after our bodies and give them nourishment and exercise.

As a teacher you must encourage your students to keep their brains hydrated. Brains need water. Water is a major part of the brain. In fact, estimates suggest that the brain is made up of at least 90 per cent water. All children will benefit from an increase in their water consumption. Dyspraxics might benefit more than most. Water will help to maximize brain function. It is also important in stressful situations like examinations and tests since we tend to perspire more under stress and the possibility of dehydration can undermine concentration. When it is such a fragile flower among dyspraxics, we must do our best to nurture and preserve it.

What we are trying to do is to modify the way the brain is working so that proper connections can be confirmed or restored. It is true that the brain can be shaped and moulded. Environmental factors will make people in Japan pronounce words in the same way and display the same inabilities with English pronunciation.

Dyspraxia

A French accent or a German one is instantly recognizable. Of course the brain can be moulded by the world it experiences, it happens all the time.

There are many different beliefs about how this can be done. There are physical exercises that some believe work. I have been told, for example, that it is important to increase the blood flow to the brain. This will help concentration. So you must push your finger and thumb lightly into the slight indentations below your collar bone on each side of the sternum. At the same time you should press gently on your navel. As a teacher, you can teach your children how to do these things for themselves.

Or how about marching while sitting down? It is suggested that this will help to coordinate the information flow between the two sides of the brain. Put your right hand across the body to the left knee as you raise it, then repeat the process with the left hand and the right knee. Do this for a couple of minutes.

By doing these things you will be confirming the connection between movement and learning, and trying to maximize achievement in both. This is the basis of educational kinesiology, which tries to stimulate a flow of information through the brain. In improving the efficiency of the different parts of the brain there can be significant improvements in conditions like ADHD and dyslexia as well as dyspraxia.

There is also interesting evidence from those who have undertaken a regime of physical exercises to improve brain function. Repeated exercises like walking heel to toe backwards and forwards or throwing a beanbag into a bin have helped some young dyspraxics improve their performance and their behaviour.

When the exercises are stopped, the problems return and remain until the exercises are resumed.

Whether these things make a genuine difference is up to others to judge. But the point must be that if they make the person believe they are working then they serve a useful purpose. We do the same when we go to the gym to maintain our bodies. Why should we treat our brains with less respect?

Other techniques are more widely accepted but in essence they are not much different. Listening to Mozart improves IQ scores. Mind maps, which are a means of presenting complex material in a visual form that identifies connections between ideas, could be an important way of helping a dyspraxic to learn. It can provide a pathway for learning. It might well reveal lost and overgrown pathways in the jungle inside our heads. The hope is that connections will be restored. It is definitely an area where there is lots going on at the moment and teachers would be well advised to keep an eye on it. As teachers, we always need to think about how we can fine-tune brain power. It will not only help your dyspraxics; it will help everyone in your classroom.

19

A Cure?

There isn't one.

But it doesn't stop lots of companies telling you that there is. Therapy clinics will tell you how they will diagnose the problem – this isn't that difficult. What is more challenging, of course, is the therapy itself.

You can see that a child can't use a pencil or a fork or can't pile bricks up. You can show that a child isn't sure where their body parts are and can't orientate themselves successfully. Now do something about it.

And that, of course, is the difficult part. Because to effect a true cure you will need to influence what is happening inside the brain. As a teacher I have been trying to do this with limited success for over thirty years.

Today they will wire a child up to a computer that will tell them lots of impressive things. Now I might be completely wrong here, cynical when I should be awash with wonder, but when I read about computers that will assess the functioning of the brain, compare the two hemispheres and then generate an appropriate treatment regime that will repair functions, I start to worry.

So, if you are still strangely sceptical, how about listening to neuro-music? Apparently, this will restore links in the brain. Of course, you could try brushing nerve endings. This will restore blockages in the nervous system. Alternatively, if you don't fancy that then we can try some drugs called psychostimulants. Don't worry, we can deal with the side effects later. And what about special booths in which you stand to expand the dormant parts of your cerebellum?

The common factor in all these miracle cures of course is that they cost money. They provide easy answers for people who are worried and vulnerable. Just go and search the Internet, you will find plenty of clinics ready to take money from worried parents. As commercial concerns they offer solutions. When you have paid large sums of money for stuff that contains a complicated-looking computer printout, perhaps you will be predisposed to believing that it will work. When you are confused and fearful, guilty that your child has an unexpected burden to carry for which you are in some way responsible, you will be prepared to believe a doctor who can explain and cure. All you need to do is to click here.

But at the moment there is no cure, so don't raise false hopes of finding one. You won't. I am not saying that you must accept the condition and do nothing about it. It is a challenge thrown down that you must take up. That is what this book is about. But at the moment there is no magic bullet. And there is no point in expecting one. Children and their parents must manage the condition and find the best way through the jungle.

Everyone has a right to expect an easier life and dyspraxia makes it more difficult than seems fair. But there should be no surrender. Fight it, master it, but do not waste time seeking out a transformation. The condition can touch you but you can't touch it physically. You can't replace the wires. All you can do is hope that the connections grow.

Developmental dyspraxia is not an illness or disease from which you can recover. It is a neurological disorder that you must learn to cope with. And there are thousands of adults with dyspraxia who have learned to compensate and to deal with their problems. Children diagnosed with the condition need to know this. It isn't new. It has always been there in one form or another.

The earlier a child is treated then the greater the chance of developing coping strategies.

All you can do is to teach the child praxis – to help them form ideas, to plan actions and to carry them out. There is no substitute for repetition and reinforcement. Some of this support might need to be specialist support. Speech and language therapists will help the child to gain control over speech muscles so that controlled and organized sounds can be produced. They would look at the shapes the lips adopt and where the tongue is placed. They will then help with the sequencing of movements. It is a slow process but improvements can and will be noted. But there is much too that a classroom teacher can do in all sectors, from pre-school right through to adolescence. Fine motor skills can be encouraged through play with toys such as puzzles and blocks in the nursery and through computer-based activities in the secondary school.

Tap into the expertise of physiotherapists. Their work can do a great deal for the promotion of self-confidence. They can make a real difference to the dyspraxic child's relationship with the rest of the world.

Dyspraxia

That is what a dyspraxic child needs most of all – a sense of esteem. They will be acutely aware that in the physical world in which we live they live underneath their own personal rain cloud.

Individual help from a teacher or a learning support assistant could be very important in maths or reading or spelling. This sort of attention from an adult will be much valued by a child who might find relationships with their peers hard to form. Always remember that they can learn, they can improve, they can achieve.

While the basic repetition of tasks will help, much in the end comes back to individual attention. Without it they could develop into frustrated and unhappy adults, becoming a permanent drain on a society's welfare and guests of our prison systems. What a horrible burden of guilt for parents who might thus feel responsible for ruining their child's life.

What we must do is to convince children with the condition that they can achieve worthwhile goals. Yes, they have a problem but it is not insurmountable. With informed understanding and proper consistent support, schools can make a real impact upon children with this unfortunate disability. And if our profession chooses to deal with it properly then it will make better teachers of us all and our schools will be more successful places. It won't just be the dyspraxic students who will benefit either.

If we judge a society on how they deal with the weakest members of that society, then shouldn't we be doing the same thing with our schools?

Children with dyspraxia are delightful and caring people who deserve our support as they wrestle to grasp the slippery eel of coordination. They have, through no fault of their own, an unfortunate set of connections in their brain. They don't need to be condemned. Indeed who knows what sort of insights these different connections might one day bring? Their brains are wired up differently, which means they can be very creative. The fact that they see connections that others do not means that they have unusual and original processes. Your job as a teacher is to uncover the gifts that they have.

They need structure and order, they need support in planning and in organizing. They need reassurance and security. If we are to provide the help they need and deserve, then we have to show sympathy and understanding. If their brains are not the same as ours then what does that matter? Who can say what is normal? Indeed if normal means average then who wants to be average? Has there ever been a greater insult? When we were teenagers, how many of us wanted to be normal?

The dyspraxic child is different and those differences need to be celebrated. The key to everything is sensitive and informed teaching. If you have read this book you have shown that these are the qualities you want to display.

Your pupils are lucky and are well on the way to getting the expert teaching they deserve. Good luck.

Resources

Two names to look out for are Madeleine Portwood and Amanda Kirby. They have done a huge amount of work to develop research into dyspraxia and to develop strategies to help children with it.

Kirby, Amanda (2003) *Dyspraxia: The Hidden Handicap*, Souvenir Press.
Kirby, Amanda and Drew, Sharon (2003) *Guide to Dyspraxia and Developmental Coordination Disorders*, David Fulton.
Portwood, Madeleine (1999) *Developmental Dyspraxia: Identification and Intervention* A Manual for Parents and Professionals, David Fulton.
— (2000) *Understanding Developmental Dyspraxia* A Textbook for Students and Professionals, David Fulton.
Other useful books are:
Boon, Maureen (2000) *Helping Children with Dyspraxia,* Jessica Kingsley.
Ripley, Kate (2001) *Dyspraxia: DCD.* A Handbook for Teachers, David Fulton.

Index

Index

Index

Index